Cultivating Peace and Hope

Cultivating Peace and Hope
Healing from Anxiety
and Depression
Through Reflection and Introspection

Anna Malebogo Choongo

For more information email: anna@annachoongo.com

ISBN: 978-0-6450599-0-8 (paperback)
ISBN: 978-0-6450599-1-5 (ebook)

Dedication

TO MY BROTHER TSHIDI
May you find peace and healing in your life. I believe in your strength and capacity. All will be well.

TO MY FAMILY
Thank you for who you are and for journeying through this life with me.

To Papa, Mum, Cecil, and Kuki, I hope your souls have found solace in the light of God. May you always rest in eternal peace. I love you all very much.

TO MY HUSBAND
Thank you for being who you are and for holding my hand through it all. I admire your strength and tenacity and cherish your love.

Contents

Introduction

This book is a memoir documenting my life experiences and how certain circumstances, including upbringing, contributed to depression and anxiety in later years of my life.

I was fortunate to grow up in a middle-class family. My parents dedicated a lot of effort to providing material comforts for us and raising us as best as they could in colonial Africa, where personal liberties for black African people were limited. Irrespective of the challenges of the time, my parents provided well for us, ensuring that my siblings and I had a good education and developed a broad, balanced view of the world and our place in it. We were exposed to many fun and enriching family experiences.

Despite the good times and upbringing, there were also tense moments between Papa and Mum, sometimes erupting into violence. This often affected the mood around our household. My own moods subsequently became regulated by the moods of my parents, and yet the subject of family violence and how it affected my siblings and me was never discussed or considered.

We were a model family in the community, and matters of family violence stayed within the household. My parents were loving and caring but experienced significant life challenges that sometimes resulted in traumatic situations for the family.

My family was not unique in this sense. This is the way that many African households functioned in those days. The father was the unquestioned head of the family who determined matters of household existence. Women were often relegated to submissive roles and endured much violence from their spouses as a form of discipline.

Using violence as a means of discipline was not confined to the household. It was widely accepted in all realms of society, including at school. In my home, my younger brother and I also experienced considerable violence at the hands of a domestic helper.

As a little child growing up in an environment often filled with fear and uncertainty, I developed a belief system that skewed my perception of the world and of other people in response to experiences that were happening around me. I internalised the belief that women were unlovable and unworthy. Exposure to domestic violence contributed to mental health challenges throughout my life. This was compounded in later years by further traumatic situations such as being severely bullied in school, mental and physical abuse by teachers, getting involved in dysfunctional relationships, and repeated, unsuccessful attempts to become a mother.

I believe these challenges thwarted my ability to reach my full potential. In time, the weight of these traumatic situations resulted in anxiety and depression. The difficulties I experienced in my childhood bring a unique perspective to this topic about the negative and long-term impact of childhood trauma on adult life.

Like many people dealing with mental health issues, I was reluctant to recognise my problem and seek help for fear of being perceived in a negative light. I was conscious of the stigma in society about mental health. I dismissed my mental conflict as everyday stress and rebelliousness. I tried hard to conform to the expectation that I should cope like everyone else. It embarrassed me even to consider I might have a problem.

However, my mental state impacted my daily decisions and choices until I could not ignore it anymore. I faced the following psychological challenges; low self-worth, overwhelmed by the struggles of routine life, and disempowerment to disclose that I was struggling.

Through my story, I share lessons I have learned about my own mental health. Taking responsibility for my journey became the key to finding the path to healing. I've often dreamed I would one day share the story of my personal experiences arising from traumatic occurrences in my life, including childhood trauma. However, I feared being judged. I worried about people's perceptions and understanding of mental health issues. Approval by others has always been a big need for me, given my background and history.

When I finally started perceiving myself consistently in a positive light, I realised sharing my story had nothing to do with people's opinion of me. I hope there are people whose life stories and experiences resonate with mine. In writing this memoir, I am honouring myself as I am. I am also celebrating my capabilities.

The book discusses the strategies I used in my battle against anxiety and depression. I learned and used these strategies over several years. While they have not "cured" the anxiety and depression, they gave me space and clarity to work towards my own healing. To me, healing involves full awareness and acceptance of self, despite personal afflictions. Awareness and acceptance lead to wisdom, growth, and holistic health. Working through anxiety and depression is a very personal journey, influenced by one's particular circumstances and lived experiences.

I am not an expert in healing mental health and depression. However, I have lived and struggled with and continue to overcome anxiety and depression. I believe sharing my experience can help others with how to deal with similar issues. This book narrates my quest to purge the past and to move ahead and live life, with all its trials, from a fresh perspective.

Preamble

In December 2019, my husband Moran and I embarked on a holiday to the UK and Norway. We needed this break after a horrific and traumatic 2018. We were now ready to travel after Moran's ill health. The stress of dealing with the ordeal of his illness landed me with severe anxiety and depression. The trip offered us the opportunity to move on and relax.

We were going to spend the holiday season in Leeds, Northern England, visiting my younger sister, Rose. Afterwards, the three of us were to travel to join a cruise along the Norwegian coast. We left Sydney for London on a hot and smoky morning, looking forward to experiencing the Northern Hemisphere winter and having a white Christmas.

We landed in London on the 18th December and spent two days enjoying the city and taking in a show at the West End. Then we flew to Manchester and caught the train to Leeds. Leeds is a cosmopolitan city, surrounded by rolling green hills and stunning countryside. It is not as hectic as London, yet it has its own pulsating vibe. I always find it stimulating and relaxing whenever I go there to visit. We had a lovely Christmas and New Year. It did not snow on Christmas day as Moran and I had expected. That was frustrating; we had wanted to experience a white Christmas.

The post-Christmas sales were great, and we did lots of shopping, stocking up on warm gear to prepare for the bitter Norwegian winter. We flew to Norway in January 2020 to board the Hurtigruten ship for a seven-night cruise from Bergen in the South to Kirkenes in the North. The

Hurtigruten fleet carries cargo and passengers along Norway's seaside towns and offers tourists a great opportunity to experience Norway's expansive coast. During the journey, passengers alight and explore the different towns where the ships dock to deliver cargo.

This was my first sailing experience. I was excited and looking forward to crossing the arctic circle and seeing the magnificent northern lights. We boarded our ship on a freezing, wet evening and set sail in choppy seas. The rough conditions raised my concerns about becoming seasick. The captain and staff assured us that the MS Nordkapp, our vessel, could handle the rough seas. We settled into our cabins, and before dinner, we went to the lecture hall to meet our fellow travelers and receive instructions about safety protocols while on board.

The first day of the trip was rough, with twelve-metre-high waves and foul weather. It was snowing, so we spent time exploring the ship's facilities and attending interesting lectures on Norway's history and culture. We lazed around, viewing unbelievable scenery as the ship sailed past majestic, snow-covered mountain ranges lining the coastline. Norway is a stunning country with amazing landscapes.

The weather calmed on the second day, giving us the opportunity to disembark and explore towns where the ship docked. I loved taking in the magnificent surroundings and experiencing the fresh atmosphere. I also enjoyed sitting at the window of my cabin, viewing the gigantic waves. I found this soothing and relaxing. As we approached the arctic circle, the sun disappeared altogether.

Three nights into the trip, I fell asleep while reflecting on how lucky I was to be undertaking this journey and had a profound dream. In my dream, I was in an extensive park, surrounded by old trees and expansive large rolling green fields. I was sitting on a bench by a tranquil, still-water pond. Little red, blue, and green coloured fish swam in the water amidst floating, bright green leaves. The sun was dazzling, making the surrounding colours even more vivid.

A soothing breeze blew on my face as I sat there wearing white pants and a matching loose shirt. I was throwing small pebbles into the pond, creating soft ripples.

I looked up from the water and saw Mum and Papa walking towards me, holding hands. They resembled young lovers on a first date. The picture was bizarre. This side of my parents was new to me. They had never displayed their love for each other in public. This sight reassured me they had overcome their struggles and were in harmony.

Behind them were my older brother Cecil and older sister Kuki. They smiled at me and said in unison, "We are so overjoyed to see you cheerful. We knew you could do it."

Mum glanced at me with a warm smile. "I am sorry, my daughter. I was not always there for you when you needed me most. Please try to understand my dilemma. I loved you so much and did not want to separate you from your Papa, whom you adored. I thought I was doing the right thing for you and did not realise the damage this would cause to your lives. Look at Cecil and Kuki, and your brother Benny." She then gazed at Papa in tenderness. "Your father did the best he could under the circumstances."

In his deep voice, Papa addressed me by my pet name, which means big ears, and said, "Mazebe, you know we love you. Life is not always easy. Sometimes we stumble, but we have to get up and follow our path. You need strength and determination to reach your destiny. I am sorry, my child, that it has been a rough road for you. But I am proud of you. You have transitioned from that little insecure and frightened girl you were when we lived in Francistown. I remember many times coming home from work to find you waiting for me to read you stories. You loved to learn, and you yearned for our love. Sometimes we fell short of giving you that care." I stared at him in amazement. It was unusual for Papa to be that expressive.

In that instant, the dream transitioned to another scene. A six-year-old young girl was sitting next to me, dressed in white. She stared at me with wistful, pure dark brown eyes. I realised she was me. "Let the sorrow go. Be joyful. Things have changed now. We're safe," I said to her.

In that moment, I experienced a profound sense of peace and harmony. I was my true, gentle, and free self and felt loved and protected.

I had a quick flashback to my early twenties, recalling the weight I always carried and my belief that my family considered me a failure. The pain of being judged for my mistakes had haunted me for the best part of my adult life. The road to accepting my life had been a hard one.

As I looked up from the little girl towards my parents, I jolted awake and sat up on the bunk bed, disoriented. The ship was rocking and humming along as I thought back on my strange dream. For a start, my parents, Cecil, and Kuki died years ago.

My dreaming of them in this way was significant, empowering, and comforting. Peacefully dreaming of Mum and Papa reflected the ideal family environment that I had always wished for while growing up.

I realised this dream helped me get in touch with my inner child and the anguish I have carried throughout my life. This dream gave me the determination and freedom to pursue my desire, which had always frightened me—the desire to tell my story.

We arrived back in Australia in late January 2020, and soon after, COVID-19 hit. We were lucky to have completed our traveling before the virus spread. As fate would have it, in July of 2020, my workplace made me redundant because of the economic impact of COVID. The redundancy gave me the space to write the book. My story starts with the events that happened one stormy night.

Chapter 1

Stormy Night

"There's a growing cohort of kids on today's university campuses who did everything 'right' at school, aced their exams, got into fancy university and find the academic work a breeze, but are completely baffled by life. They have no clue how to deal with a housemate who's a slob, or a romantic interest who just isn't that into them."

— *Susan David*

I was a naïve 18-year-old and four months into my freshman year at the University of Botswana when I met Jake and fell in love. It was October 1975.

Campus life was busy and exciting, and the weekend always brought excellent entertainment, parties, a disco, or an outside band invited to perform on campus. The dance parties took place in the campus dining hall, which was in an area that students called the entertainment precinct. It included a tuck shop and a small office, all facing inwards to a wide, grey cobblestone courtyard. The dining hall was enormous, with rectangular tables that sat several hundred students at a time. It had a commercial size kitchen with a food service area.

When there was entertainment in the hall, students stacked the tables against the wall, creating a large empty dance floor. The well-stocked tuck shop, which was opposite the dining hall, sold alcoholic and non-alcoholic drinks. Many students lingered around the tuck shop after dinner. They gathered in different social groups, sitting on the metal tables and benches spread around the courtyard, drinking alcohol and waiting for whatever entertainment was on for the night. Loud music would blare from the tuck shop's large stereo system as students sat around, waiting in anticipation.

One Friday night, there was a disco on campus. Thapelo, the most popular DJ in town, was bringing in his latest music set to perform. These nights drew many people from all over Gaborone town.

Gaborone, the capital town of Botswana, was diverse, progressive, and buzzing. It was the place where the principal Government offices were located. Many public servants and expatriates worked there in various sectors, including foreign embassies, the local hospital and health facilities, retail sectors, and schools. Most offices, the retail sector, the local cinema, and hotels were in the main town centre.

A couple of kilometres from the town centre was the African Mall, which also had retail outlets, including markets that sold local goods and produce. Both the town centre and the African mall were within walking distance from campus. Public transport was not always available in those days. Many people walked everywhere. Sometimes we hitched rides with motorists if they were travelling in the same direction we were going. There were few taxis around town.

Gaborone provided a rich cultural and social experience for the university community, as students got to interact with a diverse variety of people. Sometimes on weekends, students travelled into town for movies or parties. Entertainment on campus was popular with everybody, as the campus provided regular, high-quality entertainment.

Thapelo had the latest 70s American pop and played hits from the Commodores, Spinners, Teddy Pendergrass, Isaac Hayes, Ashford and Simpson, and Barry White. This was the "in" music of the 70s, and it sustained the "cool" campus entertainment scene. Everybody loved the music!

The excitement in the air was electric this Friday evening. We had not had a disco on campus for weeks. The government had paid us our semester stipend, so we were all cashed up and ready for a boozy night. You could feel the buzz of anticipation in the dining hall at dinner time, with various students talking about the upcoming entertainment.

My buddies Gemma, Leila, Brie, Joyce, and I rushed to our rooms after dinner to get ready for the disco. The girls and I had met on campus and hit it off. We chatted in excitement, shouting across to each other as we dressed. We had bought new clothes with the stipend and were helping each other with makeup.

Leila knew how to wear and apply makeup, and she helped me, as this evening was my first time wearing makeup. Mum did not allow it.

She walked over to my room after I finished my shower. "Have a seat over here," she gestured to a spot on the bed. I sat, and she started working her magic.

"The blue eye shadow is great with your colour and your top," she said, as she applied the makeup with brushing sweeps.

"I don't want to appear ghostlike!" I said. It was all new to me.

She laughed. "Oh, don't be silly. You look great with makeup."

My mother's disapproving voice popped into my head, *"What have you done to your face? Wipe that muck off!"* I shivered.

When Leila finished, she refused to let me have a peek. "Be patient," she said. She undid my braids, then combed and shaped my hair into the latest afro style. "All done," she said a few minutes later, as she stepped back to admire her work and gave a self-satisfied thumbs up. "Check yourself in the mirror." I stood up and walked to the floor-length mirror inside the door of my closet.

Oh my God, is that me? I thought. She had done a fantastic job. "Oh, I like this," I said, admiring myself from different angles. Apart from the blue eye shadow, which I was unsure of, I looked splendid. She grabbed my hand, and we walked across the courtyard to Gemma's room.

"Oh my. You look nice," Gemma said, looking me up and down. "Hey, Lei, can you do my hair as well?" she asked, turning to Leila. Leila got to work.

It took her a while to finish doing our makeup and hair. She was a genius with this. We finished dressing before meeting again in the courtyard.

I wore my favourite tight black bell-bottomed slacks and a white tank top. Brie adorned an elegant pair of fawn, straight cut slacks, with a long flowing black top. Gemma had on a beautiful tight cream dress that showed off her stunning full figure to perfection, and Leila wore Levi jeans with a lovely red blouse. Joyce looked smashing in a stylish red and white floral skirt with a matching top; she completed the look with a beautiful beret. We were ready to go, all wearing ridiculously high-heeled shoes and full make-up. We headed to the tuck shop for a drink before the disco started.

The scene at the tuck shop was organised chaos. The latest South African soul music was blaring from large black speakers perched on the tuck shop counter. The night was on.

"Hey girls, come on over for a dance," one bloke shouted. We ignored him and selected a pleasant, quiet spot to sit and watch the activities. He got the message and moved on to find someone else to harass.

Many guys were already tipsy, slurring words, gyrating and swaying their hips to the music in the latest dance craze. Some of them were troublemakers, and we steered clear of them. Gemma and I went to purchase drinks; our drink of choice was cheap Carafino wine. It came in large carafes to share, and it packed quite a punch. We sat and chatted for about an hour until the disco got underway.

Around eight o'clock, the tuck shop music stopped as Thapelo set up his music system to start the disco. We all rushed into the hall, drinks in hand, on to the dance floor. The hall was filling up quickly. The room soon became hot and stuffy. I strolled outside for some fresh air and sat on the courtyard wall.

I noticed Jake standing alone, a short distance from me, holding a can of Castle beer. He glanced in my direction, and our eyes met. He smiled and gave me a small wave. I smiled back, self-conscious and uncomfortable. Then he walked over. Nervous excitement rose inside me.

Oh my God, he's coming over! What will I say to him? Make nothing of it! I muttered to myself. He came and sat next to me. My attraction to him was instant.

He was about five years older than me, tall and thin, with piercing, mischievous eyes and a well-trimmed goatee. We previously attended the same high school, and he was a popular softball player. I had seen him around campus with his group of friends. They were a trendy, sophisticated group and were into jazz music. They often threw jazz parties and only invited sophisticated people. We had never spoken. He intrigued and scared me. He was way out of my league, I thought.

"Hi, Anna, right? I'm Jake," he said with a boyish and mischievous smile. Very sexy.

"Hi," I said, not quite looking him in the eye.

"Nice night, isn't it?"

"Yeah, it's great. Beautiful music."

"You were at St Joseph's, weren't you? I think you were in Form Three when I completed. How are you finding campus life?"

"So far, so good. I'm enjoying it, and I have fantastic friends!"

He realised I was nervous. He was teasing me with his eyes. *God, he was so attractive.* We chatted for a little while longer.

"Would you like to dance?" he asked.

"Sure."

We left our drinks on the courtyard wall, and he held my hand as we walked into the hall. It was impossible to hold a conversation as the music was loud. He kept smiling at me as we danced. Then he pulled me closer against his body as we swayed to a funky, slow number. I could feel the chemistry between us. He held me tighter, and I did not want him to let go. When the music stopped, we strolled back outside and sat talking for ages. I was now much more relaxed and enjoyed getting to know him.

"Would you like to come to a party with me next Saturday?" he asked.

"Oh, where about?"

"It's in town, at Nunu's. Have you met her?"

"No. I haven't."

"She's from Serowe, like me. She throws brilliant parties. You'll have fun."

"Sounds great. I'd love to," I smiled at him.

"Great. I'll pick you up from your room Saturday around eight," he said.

I gave him my room details. He walked back to join his mates, and I moved back into the hall to find my friends. I was excited and spent the rest of the night stealing glances his way. Gemma and Brie teased me, saying I was falling in love. Brie cautioned me to take it easy, as Jake and his friends were much older, and people said they were players.

I thought she was exaggerating. I was not yet adept at reading character and took everything at face value. I was impatient during the week. It passed slowly. Saturday couldn't come around soon enough.

Jake picked me up at eight the following Saturday evening. Gemma and Leila had helped me select a flattering outfit that made me look my best. The look of admiration in Jake's eyes thrilled me.

"Nunu's place is near African Mall. We'll be there in about 20 minutes," he said.

"No problem." I was nervous and excited as we walked from the campus to Nunu's.

He had his arm around my waist. I enjoyed listening to his deep, sexy voice as he shared funny episodes of life on campus. When we arrived, guys and girls were sitting on the front lawn, drinking and chatting. The pungent smell of pot lingered in the air. More people were inside the small, two bedroomed house, dancing to South African Kwela music. The atmosphere seemed very jovial.

A beautiful dark-skinned girl with large bright eyes was standing by the open door as Jake opened the gate. She rushed over with a wide smile on her face and offered me her hand.

"Hello. I'm Nunu," she said.

"Hi, I'm Anna." I smiled back. She turned towards Jake and gave him a friendly hug. I liked her. She had an open, friendly manner.

"Welcome, Anna. Would you like some wine?" she said.

"Sure. That would be nice."

She grabbed my hand as Jake and I followed her inside to the drinks corner. We walked back outside with our drinks and found a spot on the lawn. "Jake, Anna seems nice. How did you meet her?" Nunu asked. I could tell they were buddies.

"None of your business," Jake was laughing as he poked his finger into her chest. "She's from Francistown and is new on campus. That is all I'm telling you. She's more sophisticated than you, village lot," he said. Laughter all around.

The crowd at Nunu's was interesting and broad-minded. Many were refugees from South Africa. Their company was stimulating and eye-opening. The party was splendid. Some guy offered Jake and me a joint. "Would you like to try some?" Jake asked.

"No, thanks. Not for me," I replied.

Jake and I left Nunu's in the early hours of the morning. We joked around and laughed on our way back to campus. The mood between us was fantastic. We clicked. He walked me back to my room. We kissed and lingered for ages before he pulled away.

"I'll see you tomorrow evening?" he asked.

"Sure. We can catch up after dinner."

Jake and I went on a few more dates. We enjoyed each other's company and spent a lot of time together. Though I realised I was falling for him, I held back from entering a full relationship.

I was still sorting out my feelings for my previous boyfriend, Cas. The relationship was not working. We had parted acrimoniously after a big fight and had not spoken since. I was considering ending it.

The Christmas break arrived, and I left for Francistown. Jake telephoned me at home a few times. It was sometimes tricky to answer the phone when Mum was home; she eavesdropped. I missed Jake a lot and kept myself busy catching up with old friends. I also met with Cas to talk about our relationship. Our lives were heading in different directions. I broke up with him, giving me the closure I needed to take my relationship with Jake to the next level.

I had changed a lot from my short time at university. I dressed differently and started wearing makeup in front of Mum. Though she did not like it, she did not stop me. She complained my clothes were too tight. She preferred me to wear long dresses instead of slacks, which I refused to do.

I spent my holidays catching up with friends. Vee, an old high school friend, and I met as I ran some errands in town one morning.

"Hi, Anna. Wow, you seem different," she said. "All grown up and sophisticated. Even wearing make-up! I think university life agrees with you."

I laughed, "University life is great. Loads of fun, great guys, but wild. Guess what; I've met someone."

"Ah, so that explains the glow. Is he from Ghetto?" We called Francistown Ghetto.

"No, he is from Serowe. In fact, he studied at St Joseph's. You remember Jake, the softball player?"

"Oh him," she said, arching her eyebrows in surprise. "Of course, I remember him. Who wouldn't? He was so above our league. How did you two get together?"

"He approached me at a dance party. We got talking, and he asked me out. I like him, Vee. I think I'm in love with him," I said, animated.

"Sounds like you are onto a great thing. Just be careful he doesn't hurt you. I hear he is a bit of a player."

"This is different. I think he loves me."

"Sounds fantastic. I'm so happy for you."

"Thanks, Vee. How about you? What have you been up to?"

She laughed. "Like you, I've met someone I like. He's from Maun, and I think he's serious about our relationship. He's in town this week; would you like to meet him?"

"How exciting. I'd love to meet him." We parted ways after arranging to meet a couple of days later, and I continued with my shopping before heading home to make lunch for my parents.

Jake stopped by my room the day after we arrived back for the second semester in January 1976. His beaming, cheeky smile was on full display. We hugged and kissed. "God, I missed you," he said. "How was your holiday?"

"It was alright. Boring without you," I said. We walked together towards the lecture rooms.

"I'll come by after class?"

"That would be great."

He came by later that night, and we walked together to his room. His roommate was away. We sat on his bed, fingers intertwined, kissing, hugging, and nuzzling. We undressed each other and lay on the bed. We took our time, savouring each moment. He was a lot more experienced than me. The gentleness and intensity of his lovemaking took me by surprise. The sound of his deep voice, calling my name over and over, was electric. I had fallen hard, hook, line, and sinker!

"I love you, Anna."

"I love you too, Jake."

We lay on the bed staring into each other's eyes. I spent the night in his room. As I was nodding off, I sensed Jake had touched a deep chord inside me. My emotions were raw and intense.

We continued seeing each other during the semester, though not as often as I wished. We sometimes went to the movies or hung out either in his room or mine, which required some planning as we had to work around our roommates.

As our relationship progressed, I sometimes felt he kept me at arm's length and compartmentalised me from his circle of friends. Though I got along well with his friends, and they acted in a brotherly way towards me, Jake did not include me in the group.

Sometimes, he did not invite me to their parties, and I would hear rumours of wild boozy nights with girls, but I ignored them. He told me the girls were just classmates. I avoided reading anything into the rumours.

We continued seeing each other. The summer break came around, and I got ready to go home to Francistown. Jake and I said our goodbyes on a wet Wednesday morning, as I caught the bus, and he left for his home village. We kept in touch by letter and the occasional telephone call. I loved his calls and was ecstatic for days after talking to him. He came to Francistown on one occasion to visit. I was lonely without him.

After the summer holidays, I noticed Jake was aloof and pensive. *It's nothing to worry about*, I convinced myself. I suspected he was cheating on me, but I ignored that suspicion. He drank a lot and visited my room, sloshed at night. It was embarrassing, but I hesitated to challenge him, not sure how to broach the subject. I tried to bring the matter up one morning.

"You were quite drunk last night," I said.

"Yeah, it was Thabo's birthday. The boys and I had fun." He laughed it off and changed the subject, not wanting to discuss the topic further.

It was difficult to relate to him when he was like that. He seemed detached. I forced myself not to read much into the situation, choosing to believe that since it was his last year of studies, the pressure was getting to him.

Perhaps I dreaded what I might uncover if I looked close enough. I was in love with him and did not want to risk losing him. Despite his aloofness and sometimes ignoring me for days, my feelings for him kept intensifying. I imagined us getting married one day.

My feelings blinded me to the fact that, apart from our fiery passion, we had few shared interests. We lived in a parallel world where he had his friends, and I had mine.

In February 1977, I missed my period. I prayed for it to come. Nothing! Blind terror overcame me. My parents would kill me if I fell pregnant! I was also unsure of Jake's reaction. He had been acting strange and subdued for some time. I broke the news to him on a Friday evening in my room. I hesitated, not sure how to start.

"What's the problem, Anna. Are you ok? Did something happen?" he asked.

"I'm late."

"What do you mean?" he looked puzzled.

"I missed my period?"

"What?" he stared at me. "How late are you?"

"I'm not sure. I think around two months. I haven't had a period since December."

"Shit!" He stood up. He paced up and down the room, his face showing raw panic. He then squatted in front of me, his thin hands on my thighs. "Are you sure?"

"I haven't had a test yet, but I feel sick in the mornings," I said.

He stared at me. "This is a real problem. We have to do something before it's too late." His cold words sounded like bombs in my ears. A different, callous side of him was emerging. He was not taking any responsibility for the pregnancy.

My friend's warnings, which I had ignored, came back to me. "What do you mean?" I had imagined he would come up with some magic solution like, "Don't worry, honey. We'll get married. I'll handle your parents."

His response was the exact opposite. "Get rid of it. My parents will kill me if they hear about this." He was glaring at me, intimidating, and in full control.

"I'm not sure I want to do that, Jake. Maybe it's not safe to abort the baby. Perhaps I should tell my sister."

Emphatically he said, "No, no, hang on. You can't tell anyone. We have to think this over. Think of your studies. This will mess everything up." He sensed my hesitation and softened his tone a bit. "I realise this is stressful. Let's talk again tomorrow. We need to think. Ok?" I nodded. He left soon after.

I sat still, hugging my tummy, shaking, and nauseated. He had made it sound like it was all my fault. I needed him to stay and comfort me. Instead, I cried myself to sleep. I sensed a veiled threat from him, implying I needed to do what he wanted, or I'd risk losing him. I wanted to keep the baby. His reaction terrified me. I loved him very much and could not think straight. I wasn't sure which would be worse, my parents' anger or losing him.

He was cold and aloof when we met in the dining hall in the morning. He came to my room after class, tense. "Have you thought about what I said?"

"Yes. I'm afraid of getting rid of the baby, and it's wrong,"

"We have no choice. This is a mistake. You cannot go ahead with the pregnancy. Just get rid of it. Other girls do it all the time, and it's still early days." He insisted until I agreed to consider it. I just wanted him to leave, which he did. In exhaustion, I curled up and fell asleep.

His visits became infrequent after that. It hurt. After a few weeks, I confided in a friend, Marie. She said to me, "The pregnancy is a real problem. Get rid of it. Leslie did it a few months ago."

"This is scary, Marie. I'm confused,"

"I know, friend. Just see Dr Bayana at his clinic and tell him your dilemma. He has helped a few girls," she gave me a friendly hug.

The following week, I visited Dr Bayana's surgery and told him my situation. "You want to what?" he looked shocked. He examined me. "You're almost four months gone. You cannot abort this baby at this stage. It's not right. Go home and tell your parents." With that, he sent me packing with a firm warning not to try anything silly.

You idiot. How could you think this would work? I was buckling under the pressure. I did not bother to tell Jake. I knew his answer. I wanted to tell my older sister Kuki but hesitated. She was also in Gaborone, at nursing school. The thought of her telling my parents terrified me. I dared not think beyond my current dilemma.

By the time the academic year ended, I had done nothing about the situation. I got a holiday teaching job at a high school in Lobatse, a town about seventy kilometres from Gaborone. Jake completed his studies and took a teaching job at St Joseph's College.

As we said our goodbyes again, he urged me to act before it was too late. Though we were still together, things became uneasy between us. He wrote to me in Lobatse, keeping up the pressure for me to act on the pregnancy. The letter shocked me to my core. It was cold and devoid of any sense of responsibility on his part. The baby was now moving. I still couldn't bring myself to tell Kuki.

Kuki came to Lobatse to visit one afternoon. We met in town. She stared at me, scrutinising me. I knew she suspected something. She knew me better than me. "Is everything alright with you?" she asked.

Defensively I replied, "Yes, what do you mean?"

"You seem to have gained a lot of weight. Are you sure everything is alright?"

"Yes, I said I'm fine. It's nothing. Can we leave it?"

She could tell from my firm voice I was fobbing her off, so she dropped the matter. She hitched a ride back to Gaborone later. I now wish I had said something!

13

I was fence-sitting on this matter, not able to decide. I felt vulnerable and confused and thought I could not win either way. The stress became unbearable. Ironically, nature took matters into its own hands.

The gripping pain woke me on a freezing Monday night. I clutched my stomach, worried sick for the baby. Something was wrong. I sensed it. There was pressure bearing on my lower abdomen. The teacher I shared the house with had gone to spend the night at her boyfriend's, so I was alone. There was no telephone in the house.

I got up and waddled to the toilet just outside my room. I sat on the toilet and felt the blood oozing. The pain was intensifying. An icy chill coursed through me. I realised I was in trouble. At that moment, my natural maternal instinct was to protect the baby—*please, God, let the baby be ok, please!* I prayed silently, desperate. The bleeding was now a steady flow. I had to act fast. There was no time to contact anyone. I had to get to the hospital.

I dressed as quickly as I could, stopping in between contractions. I was rugged up, and I braced for the biting cold as I walked the one kilometre to Athlone hospital. The night was dark and still. I tightened my overcoat around me and hurried along the narrow, sandy shortcut.

The uneven path snaked its way between dry bushes and shrubs that cast sinister shadows in the dark. I could see the dim hospital lights in the distance ahead of me. It seemed so far away. I had to stop as each contraction hit. I keeled over and steadied myself before continuing. All I could hear were my footsteps as I crunched on the dry leaves along the footpath. I concentrated all my senses and kept praying to God to keep the baby safe. I was blind with fear and panic. Little did I realise the events of that night would change my life forever.

I arrived at the hospital maternity ward. A kind-looking nurse was dozing on a chair facing the open door. In the local Setswana language, I greeted her, "*Dumela mma*, Greetings madam."

"*Dumela ngwanaka. Go rileng?*" Greetings, my child; what's wrong?

A strong contraction hit before I could answer. She stood up and supported me. "Are you pregnant?"

"Yes."

"How far gone are you?"

"About five months."

She helped me to sit down and called out to another nurse to prepare a bed. After interviewing me, she admitted me. "Hop on the bed. I'll check what is going on."

Before I responded, another massive contraction hit me. I moaned. "Here. Undress and change into this." She handed me a white hospital gown. She settled me into bed, and she parted my legs to examine me internally. Then she pressed and prodded my tummy. "You're fully dilated, and the baby has moved into the birth canal. I'm afraid there's nothing we can do. You're going to lose the baby."

I stared at her, dumbfounded. She grabbed a few heavy pads to stop the bleeding and covered me with the bedsheet. "It's only a matter of time. We must wait. Try to get some rest," she said as she walked away.

I had not uttered a word. I was in shock, and the contractions were now frequent and strong. The baby was stillborn two hours later. I propped myself up on the pillow to look at him. He was a well-formed, beautiful boy, and his head was like Jake's. He had a light-skinned complexion like mine. I wanted to reach out and hold him, but the nurse stopped me.

"There is no point, dear. Let him go," she said.

I lay there, my eyes fixed on him, willing him to move. "My little boy," the wail came from deep inside me.

It is hard to describe the visceral feeling that engulfed me. I was inconsolable. The sense of loss and guilt was overwhelming. I felt I could have done more to protect him. The wailing would not stop, "My dear little boy!" It ran deep in my soul. The enormity of what had just happened was hitting hard.

On Tuesday morning, the nurse called the school and relayed the news to Mma Dinaka, the school Matron. Mma Dinaka was a kind, soft-spoken woman. She had welcomed me when I first arrived at the school, and we had built a great rapport. She came to the hospital in the morning and brought sandwiches, which the nurse gave to me. I ate out of politeness.

She spent a while talking to the midwife before she walked across to my bed. "How are you this morning?" she asked. She was very subdued.

"I'm fine," I said, very embarrassed.

The midwife came over. "You're ok to go this morning. Have a bed rest for at least two days and make sure you eat nourishing foods." With that, they discharged me.

Mma Dinaka and I left the hospital mid-morning. As we walked back to the school, she was quiet, not her usual talkative self.

FACING THE MUSIC

A few hours after I got back, Mma Dinaka called me to her house. Mum was on the phone. Mma Dinaka handed the receiver to me; she was cold and hostile. I realised she had spoken to Mum. I grabbed the phone from her hand.

"Hello, Mum," I said.

"Hello, Anna. How are you?" she asked.

I did not know what to say. I welled up. The lump in my throat made it hard to breathe. "I was in hospital," I said, glancing at Mma Dinaka, who was hanging around the room. My pleading eyes willed her to give me privacy. I glimpsed a glint of malice in her eyes. Nope, she would not miss the opportunity to witness my slaughter.

"What is this, I hear? Mma Dinaka rang and told us you were pregnant and have committed an abortion." Before I answered, she continued, "This is bad. Come home right away. Do you understand?"

"Yes, Mum. I was pregnant, but this was not an abortion, Mum. It was a miscarriage."

She ignored my explanation. "Your father is furious. We will deal with this when you come to Francistown."

We did not speak for much longer. I could hear how upset and disappointed she was. We agreed I would come home the following week.

You irresponsible fool, I berated myself. *You've messed up.* I don't remember much of the walk back to my house. Kuki rang me in the evening. Mum had called her to tell her what had happened. It was a relief to talk to her. She was my rock in the family and the easiest to talk to. She calmed me down and promised to come the following Tuesday. Then we would go to Francistown together.

After two days of rest, I returned to work on Thursday morning. News of what happened had gone around. The staff were polite but stayed out of my way. I met with the principal. He informed me he had spoken to Papa, who instructed him to end my contract and send me home. He gave me a week to sort out my affairs and hand over to the next teacher.

I phoned Jake to let him know what had happened. "It's for the best, Anna. Everything will be ok." I heard the relief in his voice. He asked me to come and stay with him for the weekend. I caught the late bus from Lobatse and arrived at his house on Friday evening. He seemed pleased I was there and reassured me everything had worked out for the best.

"I'm terrified to face my parents, Jake."

"I understand it's a tough situation." He tried to make me feel better. It did not work. I left his place disillusioned and hitched a ride back to Lobatse on Sunday morning. I did not see him again before I left Lobatse for Francistown.

The following Monday, I received a ten-page handwritten letter from Papa. He lambasted me for embarrassing the family and said he was ashamed to call me his child. The letter did not hide his absolute disgust and loathing. He was not one to mince his words. As I read the letter, I pictured the familiar rage on his face—narrowed eyes and protruding veins on the side of his neck. His low, measured, forceful voice had the power to reduce anyone to pulp, and he used it to perfection. This is what I feared the most. It was time to face the music.

Months later, I discovered the reason Jake had not wanted the baby. He had made another girl pregnant, which his parents knew of. The news devastated me. I felt used and worthless.

CONTEXT AND REFLECTION

In hindsight, I realise what led to this horrendous situation.

When I started university, I was young, excited, and free at last from my parents. Like many girls my age, university life gave me the freedom that I was looking for. It was fun, but my upbringing had not equipped me with sufficient knowledge of life experiences.

The seventies were a time of rebellion and self-discovery for youth in Botswana. Within this mix, I lived in two opposed worlds; the freedom offered by the university community and the world of my parents.

At home, the expectation was for me to live up to family ideals. Looking at my eighteen-year-old self now, I realise how ignorant and gullible I was. I should have seen the tell-tale signs of a relationship that is not working. However, I did not have the skills to read the signals and to respond appropriately.

I grew up naïve, vulnerable, and impressionable, and had a severe fear of challenging authority. I had neither the strength nor self-confidence to stand up for myself and was eager to please out of fear of rejection. The self-limiting belief that I was worthless and not deserving of love and respect drove me.

All this contributed to my failure to push back against intimidation and pressure.

Chapter 2

The Confrontation

"Usually, what we believe is only someone else's opinion we have incorporated into our belief systems."

—Louise Hay

Kuki came to see me in Lobatse the following Tuesday as agreed. This allowed me to have a heart to heart with her. Her calm, determined manner showed wisdom beyond her twenty-two years, and her presence calmed me.

"Why didn't you come to me?" she said. "You shouldn't have kept this to yourself." I nodded in between whimpers. She placed her arm around me. "I suspected you might be pregnant, you know, but I kept quiet after you got angry with me that afternoon in town. I should have insisted you tell me."

"I'm sorry," I said, ashamed. "Jake was pressuring me not to tell anyone."

"Well, that's just wrong. Look at what has happened. Anyway, stop being so upset. You'll have other babies. Be strong."

Her voice reassured me all would be alright. I always counted on Kuki's loving presence whenever I needed encouragement. She loved me and knew how to make me feel better. She understood my emotional struggles from childhood and never judged me. We fought a lot, but our love for each other was solid. She showered me with the motherly support Mum sometimes did not give. I handed her the letter I had received from Papa.

"It's so long," she said in surprise, counting the pages with her fingers. "Oh, my God. This is terrible!" She exclaimed as she read. "How can he write such things?" When she finished, she grabbed me and hugged me. "Try not to fret about the letter. He says awful stuff when he's angry. Sometimes he is heartless."

I nodded, trying not to smear snot on her beautiful top. "Thank you for coming with me," I said, clinging to her.

"You're most welcome." Then she turned me around to face her and wiped my tears with her fingers. "Things will turn out, okay." We chatted for hours until we fell asleep, exhausted.

She spent the night in Lobatse with me. In the morning, she prepared eggs and bread for breakfast and insisted I eat before we took off. I had no appetite.

"Come on; you need to build your strength back up." After eating, we walked to the main road and caught the bus to start the long journey home to Francistown.

The bus was full. We squeezed ourselves into a seat next to two very noisy women. They had bulky plastic bags of clothes, which they had placed on the floor in front of us, making it difficult for us to stretch our legs. I could not wait for the bus to arrive in Francistown.

Under normal circumstances, I would have enjoyed the five-hundred-kilometre trip across the country. I loved Botswana's vast, semi-arid landscapes and the friendly people in the villages along the route where the bus stopped. Today, I did not pay much attention to that.

Kuki tried her best to cheer me up. When the bus stopped at the village of Makoro, a young, local boy came onto the bus, carrying a basket full of bottles of soft drink and sweets.

"Do you want something to drink?"

I nodded, yes. "Ok. I'll have a Fanta."

Kuki called the boy over and bought a Fanta for me and a Sprite for herself. The drinks were refreshing as the bus was quite stuffy.

We were quiet most of the way, and it seemed to take the bus forever to arrive in Francistown. The town came into view as the sun was at its mid-afternoon hottest. We got off at the bus stop in town and endured the hot and dry weather as we walked the few kilometres across the railway line to our home. My legs were leaden. As I lifted the latch on the small gate in our front yard, the front door flew open to reveal Mum's anxious face. She had been waiting.

Her intense, accusatory glare said it all. I had trouble looking into her eyes. She shook our hands and beckoned us into the living room. We all sat down, and after asking if we had a pleasant journey, she turned towards me.

"Anna, can you explain what transpired in Lobatse?"

"I was pregnant, and I lost the baby."

"Do you realise how dangerous it is to abort a child? Who helped you?"

"No one, it was a miscarriage."

"That's not what Mma Dinaka told us. She claimed you had an abortion."

"That's not correct," I said.

"Are you saying Mma Dinaka is lying?"

Mum was staring at me. I was in a tricky situation. I hesitated. I did not want to accuse an elder of misleading them. I repeated my statement that I had a miscarriage, and this made her even angrier.

Kuki then interjected, "Mum, the pregnancy was a mistake. Anna does not deny that. However, we have to believe her when she says she did not abort the baby."

Mum did not wish to entertain that argument. After a long, loaded pause, she spoke. "Your father is livid. I will leave you to explain all this to him." With that, she sent me outside to talk to Papa.

Papa was sitting on his favourite picnic chair under the large mophane tree in the backyard, chatting with Uncle Adam, his younger brother, and Uncle Masetsane, his cousin. They were having a cup of tea. Papa was drinking the tea as he always did, pouring it into a saucer, blowing on it, and slurping it as he drank.

He looked relaxed as I took in his familiar physique. Papa was tall and light-skinned, of a solid build, with broad shoulders like a boxer. His hair was very short and neat, and he had a thin moustache. His confidence commanded authority and respect from all who met him.

When he was in good spirits, he was personable, kind, and funny. However, his anger often got the better of him. Everybody avoided getting on the wrong side of him. He saw me approaching and stopped talking, turning his gaze towards me.

I bowed to greet him. "Hello, Anna," he responded.

I turned to my uncles. Their faces beamed as they looked at me. "How is university?" Uncle Adam asked.

"It's good, Uncle. We are on holidays now," I said.

"It's good you have come home."

We chatted for a short while, then I excused myself and walked back into the house as Kuki came outside to greet them. My younger siblings had just arrived from playing at one of the neighbour's houses. They jumped in delight when they saw Kuki and me. They loved having us home. Kuki and I left my siblings listening to music and found a quiet spot to chat.

"I told you it would not be too bad," She said. "I think everything will go well."

My uncles left later that night after dinner. Mum summoned me to the dining room, and Kuki came with me for moral support. She shut the door.

Papa turned to face me. He snarled, "Anna, you can't imagine how stunned and embarrassed I was when the principal of Lobatse Secondary School rang me to tell me what you had done. I never expected you would do something like that."

I was quiet, not daring to maintain eye contact with either of them.

He continued, "You're lucky there were visitors when you arrived today. Otherwise, I would have slammed you against the furniture. Your behaviour is shameful."

"Who is the boy?" Mum asked.

"His name is Jake. He is from Serowe." I replied.

"Does his family know?"

"No, I don't think so."

Mum carried on, "This is bad. I want you to stop seeing him. Do you understand?"

I promised to stay away from Jake and concentrate on my studies. I felt small, shunned, and rejected. The tension in the house was unbearable until Papa departed a week later on one of his usual work trips.

Even after he left, tension remained in the house. Kuki and I were in the kitchen getting breakfast the morning after he left when Mum walked in. She addressed me, "You realise, your father is still mad at you. He declared that if you died, he would be happy to pay for your coffin."

We stared at her, speechless.

How do I respond? I stood up and ran to the bedroom, bursting into agonising sobs. How had I sunk so low? I knew I had made a mistake, but this reaction was extreme. The following days were hard as I struggled to deal with my predicament. I kept to myself and avoided annoying Mum further.

Kuki went back to nursing school. I had stayed home. My younger brother, Benny, noticed my misery and asked what was wrong. I invented a lame excuse to avoid telling him the truth.

Mum warned me before I left to go back to University for my second year. "Just remember this. If you fall pregnant again, you will stop your studies and stay home to care for your child. I will not be a carer for anyone's baby. Is that clear?"

"Yes, Mum. I understand." And that was that. I walked out the door heading to university.

University was very different this time. Jake had completed his studies and gone.

Friends tried to support me, but they could not relate to my trauma. They expected me to put everything behind and move on. So, I put on a brave face and bottled my genuine feelings to please everyone. I joined the party scene once again.

Jake called on me on a few occasions. I travelled to Kgale to visit him. My friends told me he was sleeping around, and I watched him flirt at parties. This all hurt like hell, but I turned a blind eye. How could I let him go? He had a strange hold on me.

My feelings for him ran deep, and I ignored the emotional abuse as long as he stayed with me. I hoped we would get married, and he would change.

On rare occasions, he showed up to see me; he apologised for his actions and promised to behave better. I accepted this and hoped for the best. He never kept his word, and I forgave him again and again. Soon I saw even more of his cold and uncaring side.

Jake came to see me late one afternoon, a few months before completing my second year in 1977. "Can we go for a brief walk and talk?" he asked.

His manner was cockier and more arrogant than usual. He was stroking his goatee, a sign that something irked him. I was unprepared for what came next. "Anna. I've moved on, and I want to end this relationship."

"What? Why? I thought we loved each other?" My heart was thumping hard.

He gave me a disdainful stare. "It's just not working for me. Plus, I hear stories you are the real party girl these days."

"That's not true, Jake," I pleaded. "Whoever told you that is being malicious. Can we please talk this through?"

"Nope. I have decided. There's nothing to say. Good luck to you." After that short, tense exchange, he left.

I stumbled towards my room, numb and in tears, thoughts swirling in my head. *What just happened? How did I arrive here?*

His words did not make much sense. I had tried hard; the relationship did not work out.

Severe depression set in. I attended lectures, but my heart was not in my studies. However, I still scraped through and passed my second year.

CONTEXT AND REFLECTION

I grew up believing I was unlovable and not good enough. The confrontation with Papa reinforced this belief. When Jake rejected me, I had no emotional resilience to support myself. His actions also confirmed my belief that I was not good enough.

I believed love was conditional and that I had to please others to be loveable.

This pattern endured into my adulthood and, in turn, resulted in my involvement in dysfunctional, difficult relationships.

Chapter 3

Where It All began

"When we are very little, we learn how to feel about ourselves and about life by the reactions of the adults around us."

—Louise Hay

I was born in Lobatse, a small town in the South of Botswana, about seventy kilometres from Gaborone. Lobatse is close to the border with South Africa. At the time of my birth, Botswana was a British colony called Bechuanaland Protectorate.

Under British rule, Africans lived in segregated townships away from where the expatriates lived. The town was divided by a railway line that ran across Botswana from the Cape in South Africa to Zimbabwe in the North. The railway line transported labour workers to the South African mines. Many Africans worked in low paying menial jobs as servants, gardeners, and drivers for the white people. Men and women from Lobatse crossed into South Africa, seeking work in the mines or as domestic servants. The fifties brought progress in Bechuanaland, with Batswana, as the people of Botswana are called, becoming educated and securing jobs in occupations like teaching and nursing.

My family settled in the township of Peleng, an overpopulated township sprawled on top of Lobatse hill.

Anyone driving through Lobatse could see Peleng from the main Lobatse shopping precinct across the river. Most dwellings were brown mud shacks, some with iron roofs and others with grass-thatched roofing, clustered into compounds. Families lived close to each other, sharing limited space and amenities provided by the municipality.

Our compound was on the front street, at the bottom of the hill. It had three two-bedroomed mud houses with flat iron roofing. The houses faced inwards to a clay courtyard. Those days, people plastered exterior walls and courtyard floors with a blend of cow dung and soil—the traditional African style of building—making symmetrical, colourful patterns.

Each room in our compound had a tiny square opening that served as a window, screened with colourful cotton curtains. The windows had no glass. The rooms were dark and stuffy in summer and freezing in winter. There was no power or running water. We used kerosene lamps and candles and collected water from a communal tap in the street behind our compound. There was a shared pit latrine at the rear of the yard.

We lived in an extended household. Papa, Mum, my older brother Cecil, my sister Kuki and I occupied one of the two-bedroomed dwellings. My great grandmother Mma Motshitshi, and Great Aunt Ruth—Mum's grandmother and aunt—occupied the second house. The third dwelling housed a kitchen and a makeshift bathroom.

Mma Motshitshi became Mum's guardian when Mum's mother died. Mum became an orphan at sixteen. Her father had died when she was a baby. Her only brother went to fight in the Second World War in Egypt, recruited by the British army. He never returned. When Mum's family inquired about his whereabouts, they were told no records existed. The family presumed he had died in battle.

Grandma Ruth, as we called her, preferred cooking meals out in the open courtyard if the sky was clear. The small kitchen often filled up with smoke from the open fire, making us cough and stinging our eyes.

I have rich memories of Grandma Ruth coming downhill, the morning sun shining on her thin, slender frame as she balanced a bucket of water on her head. She made a few of these trips daily as she collected enough water to fill the barrel outside the kitchen, ensuring there was ample supply for bathing and cooking. She did most of the cooking, though Mum helped on the weekend.

Other extended family members lived in different areas around Peleng and visited each other daily. On weekends, they gathered at our house to sit under the gigantic tree in front of the yard, enjoying the cool breeze and drinking skorkian, the potent local brew. They sang and joked about, with men sharing stories of their experiences working as labourers in the gold mines in South Africa.

Mum and Papa were not typical of people in Peleng. Papa had come to Lobatse for work. He was from Bobonong, a village in the central part of Botswana. He trained to be a primary school teacher in South Africa. When he completed his studies, he got a teaching position at St Teresa's primary school, run by the Catholic diocese. Many people in the community respected him. He met Mum soon after locating to Lobatse, and they married in 1953.

Mum was a nurse at the British-run Athlone Hospital. When my parents met, Mum already had a son, my stepbrother, Cecil. Cecil was six years old when Papa and mum got married. In 1954, my sister Kuki was born. Kuki was of slight build and had a slender body. I came along in 1957. I'm told I was a big, chubby baby.

My parents had done well for themselves. A few months after I was born, Mum bought a car, a Vauxhall, from an expatriate British family who were moving back to England. She was one of the few women in Botswana who drove in those days. I understand she was quite progressive at the time and took part in establishing the Nurses Association in Lobatse.

My younger brother Benny was born in 1959. He was a bubbly, outgoing and happy child. From his long limbs, you could tell he would grow to be tall. Mum's relatives showered my siblings and me with a lot of love. We felt a great sense of protection and safety, growing up within an extended family.

Though my first name was Anna, I also had several other affectionate pet names bestowed upon me by my family. Mum's family gave me the pet name of "Rami,"—Rami was short for Maramane, which means fat cheeks, and I hated the name as it embarrassed me; I cried and argued to no avail against being called Maramane. The name stuck.

Papa called me "Mazebe," which means big ears, and Cecil called me "Spona," whose meaning I never established—Cecil said he did not know what it meant, but he liked the name for me, anyway; so, it stayed! I was to gain more nicknames as I grew up.

Kuki and Cecil attended primary school at St Teresa's, while Benny and I stayed home under the care of my great grandmother and great aunt. On Sundays, we all either walked or drove to the Catholic Church at St Teresa's. I always held onto Papa's hand as we walked.

Mum's family did not like Papa much. They thought he was not suitable for her. They hated his ferocious temper, which came out in the open if anyone angered him, including Mum. Many of Mum's relatives were outspoken and intervened to defend her when necessary. I came to learn later that they thought he was holding her back from achieving her ambition.

RELOCATING TO FRANCISTOWN

In 1961, Papa got a job as a primary school principal in Francistown, a town in the North-Eastern part of Botswana, about five hundred kilometres from Lobatse. He seized the opportunity to move our family as far away from Mum's relatives as possible. I was four years old.

We packed into the small, cream-coloured Vauxhall car early one morning to make the long journey up north. The tiny car boot was jam-packed with luggage. Thick ropes secured the mattresses, blankets, and trunks to the car roof.

As we piled into the car, excited and looking forward to the journey, we were also sad to be leaving our relatives behind.

Mum and Papa jumped into the front, and we children shared the back seat. Benny and I sat in the middle, flanked by Cecil and Kuki on each side. Papa guided the laden car down the narrow, rough, dirt road from Peleng to join the main road to Francistown. We opened the car windows to let in the cool breeze.

The main road to the north was rough and sandy, an unsealed road with large potholes. Long grass and bushes lined the sides, creating a narrow corridor that accommodated only one car. At one stage, the car got bogged in the sand. We got out to push while Papa manoeuvred the wheels out of the sand. Whenever a wheel hit a pothole, the car bobbed up and down, swerving off the road. We clung on for dear life.

We passed many animals as we drove; over time, we stopped to watch deer, wildebeest, and zebras either grazing nearby or crossing the road. We were excited by ostriches running alongside the car. The animals looked beautiful and colourful amongst the shrubs and bushes.

"Are there any lions?" I asked.

"Not around here. Lions avoid coming close to populated areas. They prefer to live in thick forest. They are dangerous, so we don't want to run into them," Papa said.

Fear coursed through me as I imagined us running into lions and leopards. Cars were few on the road, and dwellings scattered, so there was not much chance of someone rescuing us.

Sometimes unattended cattle, donkeys, and goats lay on the road. They belonged to people who lived in the surrounding areas. Papa had to blow the car horn long and hard to move them along. Some cattle had tinkling bells tied around their neck, and you could hear them from afar. Papa was careful not to hit any animals.

Barefooted herdsmen tended the cattle, grey blankets draped around their torsos, their whistles piercing the quiet air to round up the livestock.

After a few hours of travelling, we stopped in Artesia. It was a small settlement close to the road and had a train station. The sun was boiling, and we welcomed the opportunity to rest. We had only had one brief stop in Gaborone a few hours earlier to top up petrol and water.

"Time to stretch your legs and go to the bushes," Papa said to us. We scampered out of the car and dashed to the bushes to relieve ourselves.

The countryside was arid, with the long dry grass providing a haven for snakes. I ran towards a small green thorn bush and pulled down my pants to wee. I heard a whooshing movement behind me, close to where I was squatting. I whirled around and saw a small, black snake slithering in the red, hot soil towards the bush where I squatted. It was moving fast. I screamed in terror and bolted back towards the car. I tripped on my pants, which were around my ankles, and scraped my knees. I stood up and continued running, screaming, "Snake, snake," at the top of my lungs.

Cecil came running towards me and asked me where I had seen the snake. I pointed towards the tree. The snake had coiled itself under the shrub. He dragged me away and helped to pull my pants up. I was shaking in terror. Mum rushed over with some Dettol, which she always carried in her luggage, and cleaned my scraped, bleeding knees.

"Always look around before you squat," she said. She took my hand and led me towards a different bush to wee. Nothing came out. She gave up, and we walked back to the car. "We'll stop later when you have calmed down," she said.

After the loo stop, we ate the provision of chicken and fat cakes that Grandma Ruth had packed, flushed down with lukewarm tea that Papa always carried in a flask. I made sure I stayed very close to the car and scanned my surroundings as we ate.

After eating, we packed up the lunch dishes and resumed the trip. Papa took his time, careful to avoid accidents with wildlife and to manage the rough road.

The sun was relentless, and the car had no air-conditioning. Hot air blew in, and the cramped back seat, which the four of us shared, was uncomfortable. I just wished we could arrive in Francistown. The novelty of travel was wearing thin.

I dozed off. "Stop leaning on me! You're heavy," Kuki shoved me off.

I was gearing myself to shove her right back when we spotted something in the distance approaching from the opposite direction. Excitement! We strained to peer through the windscreen. Yep, we could see the unmistakable thin dust trail behind the moving object.

Soon, we heard the noise of a vehicle, and an army green, old Land Rover truck came roaring around the corner. I was now standing upright and wide awake! Papa manoeuvred the Vauxhall off the road. He stopped the car, leaned out of the window, and flagged the Land Rover down. It came to a screeching, dusty halt beside us.

The driver was a heavy-set, sunburned Afrikaner—a white South African man of Dutch descent—travelling on his own. His windows were wide open, and you could see beads of sweat on his forehead. In those days, white people were not always friendly to Africans, so his stopping to speak to Papa intrigued us. Papa got out of the car. So did the man, leaving his truck running.

"*Dumela rra,*" Greetings, sir. "Where are you travelling from?" Papa asked, shaking the man's hand.

He replied in fluent Setswana, the language of Batswana people, "*Dumela rra.* I am from Mahalapye." Mahalapye was a village ahead, where we were heading.

He peered inside the car, smiled at us, and gave us a small wave. I fought hard not to burst out laughing. The man had large buck teeth, and some front ones were missing. The tobacco he was chewing had discoloured his teeth a blackish yellow, making him look comical when he smiled. He had a thin mop of wiry, reddish hair, which was brushed backward, revealing a receding hairline. Kuki was also struggling to contain her laughter. I could not stop staring. Little Benny cowered from him and held onto Cecil.

The man walked around the car, curious. "Where are you headed?" he asked.

"We're on our way to Francistown. How is the road ahead? Any rains?" Papa asked.

"Not before Mahalapye. There are many animals on the road. I almost hit an ostrich about five miles from here," he said, turning to the side and spitting a thick gob of black saliva. "Rain fell beyond Mahalapye, towards Palapye yesterday. The road is wet and muddy. Be careful." He looked at the car again, sizing it.

The rains wreaked havoc on the unsealed roads, causing widespread flooding. Roads turned into muddy slush, and railway tracks got washed away, causing train derailment.

During the rainy season, rivers overflowed, and since few, if any bridges existed, crossing the rivers after a rain was dangerous. Vehicles got bogged or washed away when it rained, hence papa's eagerness to find out if it had rained ahead. Travellers were sometimes stranded for days on the road, waiting for floodwaters to subside.

"Thank you, *rra*. I'll be careful. We also saw many animals along the way, some of them lying on the road," Papa said.

"Yes. I know the road between here and Gaborone is full of animals. Anyway, take your time and avoid driving at night between Mahalapye and Palapye. It might be a good idea to stay overnight in Mahalapye," the man said as he was getting ready to leave.

He shook Papa's hand again, jumped back into his Land Rover, revved it, and drove off, covering us with a hail of dust. We were all impressed.

The ease with which Papa spoke with the Afrikaner man made us very proud. Papa was strong, confident, and outgoing. He was very personable and knowledgeable and not afraid to converse with anyone. He respected other people and expected the same of them. He was also not afraid to confront people who did not show him respect.

We arrived in Mahalapye in the late afternoon, exhausted, and we stopped for the night. Mahalapye had a sparse population, with dwellings scattered a fair way from each other.

Papa decided it was safest to camp close to the railway station; the area was well lit by the railway station lights. The stationmaster lived in a small white brick house by the station, and he generously gave us access to boiling water for tea. We huddled in the car overnight. It was dangerous to sleep on the ground because of snakes and scorpions.

Papa woke up before any of us. "Mazebe, let's go and get some water for tea," I sat up, threw off the thin blanket the four of us shared and shoved Kuki out of the way as I flung the door open and jumped out. I followed, hopping along behind Papa as he hurried along the narrow, red, sandy path towards the nearby stationmaster's house.

These small, intimate moments with Papa were precious to me. I always wanted him to pick me to accompany him. I loved observing how he related to people and the respect he commanded. This made me proud of him.

"*Koko*," he knocked on the door when we got to the house.

The station master opened the door, inviting us in, "*Ee tsenang*, come in. *Dumela rra*," he greeted Papa.

"*Ee dumela rra*. We came to ask for some boiling water for tea," Papa said, handing over the flask he was carrying.

The man took the flask. He walked to a small paraffin stove in the corner of his kitchen and filled the flask.

He offered us to use his tiny bathroom to wash, which my father accepted with gratitude. I ran back to the car to call the others over. After brushing our teeth and washing our faces, we settled down to a breakfast of hot tea and bread that the man had sent his son to buy from a nearby store.

Such was the hospitality of Batswana people in those days. The stationmaster treated us like family. He assured us the road ahead was drivable. He had heard this from the train drivers, who were always on the lookout after it rained. We left Mahalapye before the sun got too hot and continued our journey north. Papa stopped at the store to buy drinks and biscuits.

CONTEXT AND REFLECTION

During the formative years of my life, my behaviour was influenced by the reactions of adults around me.

The extended family environment I grew up in gave me a great sense of protection and safety. I loved my parents, and I had total belief in them and would do anything to please them and make them proud of me. As a young girl, I was impressionable.

Chapter 4

New Beginnings

"We learn our belief systems as very little children, and then we move through life creating experiences to match our beliefs."

—Louise Hay

After two long days on the road, we reached Francistown in the late afternoon.

The British founded Francistown in 1897 as a gold mining town and administered it under the Tati Concession Company. The railway line from the Cape ran through the middle of the town. As was usual at the time, the British segregated the town, and the African population lived on the western side of the railway line. Whites and Indians lived on the eastern side. The African people experienced subjugation, racial discrimination, and dispossession of land.

The Vauxhall had performed well. We had stopped a few times for petrol and to check for punctures. When we arrived, we stopped in town to ask for directions. An African man gave us directions to the African School. As the name suggests, the African School catered to the local African population. The school was in the western part of town, in the area designated for Africans.

We drove across the railway line towards the school. The car bobbed up and down on the rocky gravel road as we hit large potholes. We held on tight to each other to avoid crashing our heads on the top of the car. Before us lay sparse open country, with fertile red soil, small prickly shrubs, and cactus forests. The loud shrill of cicadas pierced the afternoon air. I leaned against Kuki to peer at the cattle and goats grazing away. It was all different from the buzz of Peleng.

We saw very dark-skinned people standing by the road, speaking to one another in a strange language. It was my first time to see Africans that dark, and they scared me.

Africans in the Southern part of Botswana, around Lobatse, were lighter-skinned. The people on the side of the road stared at the car as we drove past. Papa explained that they were Kalanga people, who were the majority in the North-East district. It was all strange, and I missed Peleng, my great-grandma, and Grandma Ruth.

The school complex came into sight. "That's an impressive school," Kuki exclaimed, pointing to the white brick school buildings about two hundred metres away. "Is that your school, Papa?" she asked.

"Yes, my daughter. I believe that is it. It looks bigger than St Teresa's," Papa said, examining the neighbourhood.

The road reached a fork. One track led towards the main school complex and the other towards some white brick homes. We took the track to the brick homes.

Seven small houses stood in a row. They had flat, shiny metal roofs and were in various stages of disrepair. Their original paint was white, but it had turned a dirty red from the surrounding soil. The houses were close to each other, with no fencing between them. Most of them had overgrown vegetation around the yards.

We all checked out the area with lots of interest. A narrow footpath led from the houses to the schoolyard. Overgrown tall grass overhung the road, making it scary as if it would swallow you. I shuddered as I imagined a snake shooting from the grass as people walked through.

We stopped beside two well-dressed men sitting under a tree outside one house. They stood up and approached us. We all got out of the car.

"*Dumelang borra*," greetings gentlemen, Papa said to them.

"*Dumela rra*," they said in unison, taking turns to shake his hand. "Welcome. We have been expecting you, Rre Manyeula. How was the journey?" one man asked.

"We travelled fine. Thank God there was no rain," Papa replied. They were both looking at the car, seeming quite impressed.

The man continued, "I am Rre Phala, and this is Rre Tumelo," he gestured at the other man. "We are both teachers at the African School. It's a relief to be getting an African principal. We have been praying for that," Rre Tumelo said.

"Thank you, *rra*," Papa said. "It's a massive job, but I am looking forward to it."

The men shook Mum's hand and greeted us children without shaking our hands. They ushered us towards the tranquil shade of the tree.

A woman approached from the house and was introduced as the wife of Rre Phala. After shaking hands with Papa and Mum, she went back inside and brought chairs for them. She also brought a straw mat for us kids to sit on. We pushed and shoved each other as we jostled for space on the mat and only stopped when Mum gave us a stern look.

The woman then brought some tin mugs to serve us chilled water from a sack hung on a branch under the tree; hanging a bag from a tree like this was popular for keeping water cool during hot days. She disappeared back inside and returned with a tray laden with teacups and saucers, a steaming pot of tea, and a plate of fat cakes.

I was ravenous, and I loved fat cakes. These looked fresh and were enormous! They smelled delicious. It was hard to contain myself. I wanted to tuck in, but I knew we had to wait for Mum's permission to eat.

Mum gave each one of us a fat cake and poured some tea for us in the tin mugs. I savoured every mouthful of the warm fat cake but had to wait for the tea to cool down before drinking it. After we finished eating, the men handed the house keys to Papa and walked with us to our new home.

The house was about fifty metres from the rest, and bigger. It had a fence with a trimmed rubber tree hedge around it. The exterior walls of the house were the same dirty red as the others. However, this house looked quite nice, with a well-maintained small garden. It had two small bedrooms, a dining room, a basic bathroom, and a small kitchen with a small paraffin stove and rickety cupboard. A pit latrine stood at the rear of the yard.

"This is so nice," Kuki said as we explored the house. It was an absolute luxury compared to Peleng. The house had no electricity or running water. There was a tap in the yard which provided water for bathing and cooking. Mum and Papa liked the new place. It was spotless, and someone had left a full bucket of water in the bathroom.

We took turns freshening up before sitting down to a dinner of mealie meal and goat stew, supplied by Mma Phala. After dinner, we settled in for an early night.

Mum and Papa occupied the larger of the two bedrooms, with its two modest single beds and mattresses. Cecil slept in the second bedroom. Kuki and I slept on hide-skin mats on the dining room floor, while Benny shared Mum and Papa's room.

In the following weeks, we started exploring our new neighbourhood. We became friends with other kids who lived in our vicinity. Many African people lived further west from the school across the Tati river, in crowded shanty areas called locations, with many mud huts. The locations had no amenities and sanitation. People used the river as a toilet. The smell of raw human waste was often quite overpowering when we walked across the river to explore the locations.

Near the African School was a small store owned by a local African, where we got our groceries. No entertainment or leisurely places were available for the African people, except for a large, dirty beer hall, close to the school, where the whites sold alcohol to the Africans. Some of the local people gathered at the beer hall on most evenings, sharing stories and singing local Setswana songs. Papa and his fellow teachers shunned the place. They considered it unsophisticated and unruly.

The beer hall was also a popular place for WENELA migrant workers from the neighbouring country of Malawi. They often stopped in Francistown in transit to work as cheap labour in the mines in South Africa.

WENELA (Witwatersrand Native Labour Association) was a South African recruitment agency set up by the gold mines to recruit migrant workers. It established recruitment branches in countries across Southern Africa. The company had a large airbase on the western edge of Francistown, roughly five hundred metres from the African locations.

It was an enormous airbase, with a gigantic hangar. It attracted a lot of attention from the local African people, as it was the only structure of its kind in town. The airbase had a large perimeter fence around it. Entry to the site was manned around the clock. Only authorised people could enter.

Whenever local people heard a WENELA plane approaching the airbase, they rushed to stand by the fence, watching the plane land and the men disembark. The planes usually arrived mid-morning or late afternoon, twice a week. These were large planes, capable of carrying over a hundred people. The men spent a few days in purpose-built barracks in Francistown before being transported by rail to Johannesburg, South Africa. Huge trucks ferried them from the airbase to the barracks.

The Malawian men did not speak any Setswana, the local language. The Batswana people ridiculed them and considered them backward; people called them "Magongongo," a derogatory term, depicting how they spoke.

The migrant workers loved sitting outside the hall, drinking local beer and singing in Nyanja, one of their languages. Local boys used to harass the men. Some would pick their pockets. Others, like my brother Cecil and his friend Sam, liked to dress in long, dark coats and balaclavas and threaten the men into giving them money. They knew the migrant workers received a generous allowance from WENELA. The boys used the money to buy sweets and other treats from the local grocery store.

Cecil and Sam considered themselves to be "Tsotsis," young, urban criminals. The concept of being a Tsotsi originated in the urban South African townships in Johannesburg. Tsotsis had a distinct style of walking and dressing and carried weapons. They were sophisticated and "cool."

Whenever a plane arrived, Sam would arrive at our home in the afternoon, saying to Cecil, "Let's go to the hall and frighten Magongongo tonight. They must be rich!"

"Sure, bro. I'll wait until my parents go to bed. Have you got the weapons?"

"Yes, I'll bring a knife and a hammer. Just make sure you have your coat and face cover. I'll whistle as I approach your gate."

Cecil and Sam were both lanky and wore coats inherited from Papa and Sam's uncle. The coats were oversized and reached down to their feet, making them look like scarecrows. Like Cecil and Sam, many boys carried knives and "knobkerries," a club used as a weapon, to threaten the migrant workers. They never harmed the men, though. They knew they would end up in jail. The poor Malawians would end up parting with their pocket money just to stay safe. Fights sometimes broke out as the men tried to defend themselves.

Many of the poor people in Francistown, who could not afford to drink at the beer hall, established their own illegal beer spots in the locations called "shebeens." The shebeens sold various local brews, some of which were pretty potent and dangerous. The shebeens were chaotic and unruly places. Sometimes there were rumours of stabbings there. The police often raided the shebeens, closing them down, but they soon mushroomed again elsewhere.

Francistown town centre comprised only one main street with shops and two hotels, the Grand Hotel and the Tati Hotel, run by the whites and Indians. The hotel owners had barred Black people from entering the hotels. When a bioscope film was showing at the Grand hotel on a Friday evening, some black people came and stood outside, watching the film through the wide-open doors.

Given the racial oppression of the time, Francistown became a haven for Pan-African and nationalistic politics. The South African National Congress and the Pan-African Congress political members who had escaped the apartheid system in South Africa for security reasons settled in different parts of Botswana. They influenced the emergence of nationalistic politics. Many liberation fighters on transit to countries to the north of Botswana like Zambia and Tanzania met in Francistown as it was far away from South Africa.

The town became home to the militant and vocal Bechuanaland People's Party, which fought for the land rights of Africans in the North-East District. The Africans had been dispossessed of their land during colonisation. The party held many public rallies recruiting and urging people to join the movement fighting for the emancipation of black people. The party leaders' loudspeakers, affixed to a roving truck, often pierced the quiet evenings, announcing a party gathering on the weekend.

"*Lefatshe*, land!" the voice would boom from the loudspeaker.

"*La rona*, ours!" local people would shout in unison, rushing towards the road to watch the truck drive past.

I loved hearing this. I was learning about the importance of human rights.

As the local school principal, the party considered Papa to be in an ideal position to help recruit the locals to become party members. Papa was reluctant to oblige and also refused to join the party. He preferred to stay impartial due to his position. I believe he also did not agree with some of the party's ideologies and antics.

One day, a teacher informed Papa that the party leader had spoken of him at a rally, accusing him of not being patriotic enough.

Papa was livid, "If I see that Daniel on the streets, I'll run him over. How dare he speak about me like that!"

Within this climate of change and era of active political awakening, my family settled in Francistown. The political activities of that time affected how we grew up. They influenced our subsequent outlook on life. We were learning about fighting for and preserving our civil liberties as African people.

Papa was not a political activist. However, he had strong views about the rights of his fellow Africans. He did not shy away from expressing them. People consulted him about the problems they had in the community.

Life at home was vibrant. Many friends and relatives used to come and visit us. My grandmother Mma Paya, Papa's mum, came to stay on many occasions. I loved my grandmother very much and loved sitting on her lap. I was given the name Mma Paya, after her. It is customary in Setswana culture to name children after adult relatives. My paternal uncles and aunts fondly called me "mum".

Grandma Mma Paya used to weave beautiful skirts for me, made from a combination of yarn and colourful beads. I loved wearing them, especially in hot weather as they were light. She also bought us dried sweet reed, which was a delicacy. I used to follow her around the yard all day, helping out as she performed chores.

In the evenings, Papa's relatives, who lived locally, came to visit grandma. I would sit on her lap, listening to stories of the village where Papa grew up and what used to happen those times. I was always interested in hearing stories about how Papa grew up, and I would quiz him afterwards to get more information.

"Papa, did you say you did not grow up with grandma?"

"Yes, my child. In those days, we boys lived in the cattle post and herded cattle. The cattle posts were far from populated areas, in a dense forest with lions and other dangerous animals. Your grandmother had to stay back in Bobonong, so we were lucky if we saw her twice a year," he said.

"That's very sad. Who looked after you then?"

"I lived with your two uncles, my brothers RaMotlhabi and Adam. We lived with a distant uncle, a very cruel man."

"Did he beat you?"

"Oh, yes, almost daily. He woke us up very early, in the dark, to drive the cattle to graze. He lashed us if any of the cattle went missing. It was a challenging and dangerous life."

"Who cooked for you, Papa?"

"I did most of the cooking. Sometimes RaMotlhabi took over. When I cooked stiff porridge, he would roll some of it into a small, fist-sized ball and throw it into a large bucket full of milk. He demanded that Adam and I drink the whole bucketful before we ate the piece of porridge at the bottom. That was hard. If we didn't drink all the milk, he would flog us with a sjambok, a stiff whip made of hide."

Often, Papa and his relatives would relate many shocking stories of the hardship and suffering they endured while growing up. Those stories filled me with rage and sadness. Papa's stories also explained why he was so close to his brothers, especially uncle Adam.

MMAMORITSHANA

Kuki started school at the African School, and Cecil went to boarding high school at Moeng College, about three hundred kilometres away from home. He looked forward to going to college, but we cried when he left. My parents drove him to Moeng in the Vauxhall. Benny and I were too young to start school. We stayed home, cared for by Mma Mosibodi, a kind older woman hired to wash, clean, cook, and care for us. She always wore a bluish pinafore, bound around her large waist, with a matching headdress as was the tradition.

Mma Mosibodi was a superb cook. She treated Benny and me as her own children and reminded me of my great grandmother Mma Motshitshi in Peleng. Soon the workload became too heavy for her, and in early 1962, my parents hired an additional maid, Mmamoritshana, who was much younger, very dark, tall, and thin. She had shifty small eyes and a kind of cynical smile that she only showed when my parents were present.

Her role was to care for Benny and me. Benny and I did not like her. She ignored us and chatted with Mma Mosibodi, helping to hand wash laundry. She only called us for lunch, usually mealie rice and stew. Afterwards, she would say, "You have had your food, now go out and play."

I enjoyed playing with other local children, but Benny, who was only three, needed more attention and care. Many times, he cried for attention when he hurt himself playing. Mmamoritshana would yell at him to shut up. Benny got angry when she neglected or punished us.

One day Mum caught Mma Mosibodi concealing pieces of left-over meat under her pinafore to take home. She fired her. Once she was in charge, Mmamoritshana's real meanness showed.

She often pummelled us with her fists at the slightest excuse. She terrified us, but Benny often got furious and tried to fight back. At five years old, I was helpless to protect him. He screamed in pain as she either lashed or pinched him and twisted his arm behind his back. Then she would approach me, pointing a menacing finger at me. "If any of you dare tell any lies about being beaten, I'll show you who I am." We did not tell.

Benny developed a pattern of insulting Mmamoritshana whenever my parents were home. "Get out of here. I hate you. I wish you die." He uttered many profanities at her.

Mum tried to stop him by scolding him for saying such nasty things. He refused to stop, even with Papa threatening to smack him.

"Benny, stop," I often implored him, knowing the consequences of his actions, to no avail. This was his moment to release his pent-up fury.

Benny and I used to get stressed in the morning. "Mama, please don't go to work today," Benny screamed one morning, holding onto Mum's uniform. "Don't leave us alone with her."

Mum tried to calm him, but he held on even tighter. Mum asked Mmamoritshana to take him. The cynical, sadistic smile on her face spelled trouble. Poor Benny ran behind the Vauxhall in tears until it disappeared. Then he walked back, whimpering and defeated, knowing what was coming.

The taunts started, "repeat what you said to me last night," she said. She hit him hard across the face. She had a derogatory nickname for him, silly goat. "Come on, *matintapudi*, let's hear the names again."

I tried to come in between them to protect Benny. She slapped my face hard and shoved me out of the way. She pummelled him with her fists. Benny and I wet our pants in terror.

Today was different. She looked frightening. She came back towards us. She lifted Benny up in the air and threw him down as hard as she could. He hollered like a little hurt animal and ran outside to hide. She then stopped beating us and walked away, ignoring us for the entire day. No lunch.

Benny was whimpering and holding his arm all day, and try as I might, I could not calm him down. I could see she had hurt him. I sat with him until Mum and Papa came back home late in the afternoon.

In the evening, as we were sitting on the floor beside the table, as usual, having dinner, Mum noticed something was very wrong. Benny would not eat. He was miserable and whiny and holding onto his left arm. "Don't touch me," he screamed when Mum and Papa came close to him.

"Come on, Benny. Why are you holding your arm like that? Let me see," Mum forced him to show her. She noticed the broken arm. They drove him to the hospital, and he came back with his arm in a plaster.

"Maramane, what happened to your brother?" Mum asked me.

When I, in absolute terror, revealed the whole truth, her eyes glinted in anger. "Naughty girl. Why did you not tell us?"

I wept. I felt sad and guilty about what had happened to Benny. I felt it was my fault. She could be very harsh that way, my mother. It fascinates me now that I received the blame, yet my parents failed to pick up any clues of the abuse happening to us.

Mmamoritshana disappeared after that incident. Papa was beside himself with anger. He hunted her down but was told she had left for her home village. He never found her. Things got much better after Mmamoritshana left. We got a new, kinder maid. Papa came home a few times during the day to check on us.

ANOTHER SHOCKING EXPERIENCE

The sound of glass smashing against the wall jolted me awake one morning. I had spent the night in my parent's bedroom as I had a fever. I was sleeping in Benny's cot. Benny was sleeping in the dining room with Kuki.

I opened my eyes and struggled to sit up. I saw Papa standing across the room from Mum. He was by the dressing table, which had bottles of medicine on it.

Papa was picking each bottle and hurling it with substantial force across the room at Mum. I could see Mum through the large mirror of the dressing table. She looked petrified.

She had been getting ready to go to work. She was only wearing the pink floral petticoat that she wore under her work uniform. Mum was doing her best to avoid the missiles as they came flying at her, one after another.

Papa was wearing a white vest and brown pleated trousers tied with a thin black leather belt. His belly protruded from under the belt. He looked fixated and almost detached from his action. Whenever he was furious, his eyes became bloodshot and small, and he did not maintain eye contact. He withdrew into himself. He was terrifying.

In between ducking, Mum glanced in my direction and realised I was awake and watching what was happening. "Rra Kuki, stop!" she yelled.

He ignored her and continued flinging the bottles at her with great force. The smashing sound against the wall made my body jerk in shock. I noticed Papa's intense, uncontrollable rage. He only stopped when the bottles finished. The wall was a slithering, wet, and flowing mess of a milky white combination of medicines—the room smelt like a hospital dispensary.

Mum bolted out of the room, yelling to Cecil to call the neighbour. I had stuffed my thumb into my mouth to stop myself from screaming. I dared not move. My eyes were large orbs as I followed Papa's every movement around the room. He paced about like a caged lion, his chest heaving, and stood still as if in a trance. He then stormed out of the room, his eyes dark with rage. I heard a loud commotion in the dining-room.

One teacher, Rre Matona, a relative of Papa who lived nearby, arrived with Cecil. He tried to calm the situation.

I scrambled out of the cot, landing hard on the concrete floor as I scurried to the door in tears. Papa was now in the living room, glaring at Mum, who stood next to Rre Matona, trying to relate what happened.

She turned and saw me. "Rami, follow the other children outside."

I saw how upset she was. I ran outside to Cecil and clung to him. "Don't worry, Spona. It will be alright. Stop crying." We stood there, straining and watching through the open dining-room door.

Rre Matona tried his best to quell the tension. Papa was curt as he reassured him that the misunderstanding was over. Rre Matona left shortly after.

We came back into the house after Rre Matona left. Papa charged back into the bedroom to finish dressing. He came out, grabbed his worn leather work bag, and stormed out of the house without saying a word to anyone.

Mum tried her best to calm us down.

Cecil was furious. "Why does he do this?"

Using her pet name for Cecil, Mum, still shaken, said, "It's alright, Cisco. Leave it alone. Don't upset the little ones." That morning, she walked to work. The little Vauxhall stood in the scorching sun all day.

That evening when Papa came home, I scanned his face. It was dark, and he looked like a stranger. He walked straight to the bedroom and slammed the door behind him. Mum arrived and, after talking to me a bit, walked to their bedroom.

I could hear them arguing in there. I hated these incidents of violence. They caused incredible tension and terrible energy in the house for days, sometimes even weeks.

Neighbours tried to steer clear of intervening in our parents' issues because Papa's fury terrified them. He was also their boss, so this made the whole situation very tricky for them.

Many times, when the violence happened, I saw the resigned look on Mum's face as no one helped her. My heart broke for her, even at that young age.

One evening after dinner, an argument broke out. Mum had asked if great-grandma Mma Motshitshi could come and visit. Papa did not agree. He disliked Mma Motshitshi and thought she was a troublemaker. On this evening, we were all sitting in the dining room, having dinner. Mum and Papa were seated at the dining table, and Cecil, Kuki, Benny, and I were sitting on the floor.

We heard a whoosh and a smash. Mum screamed. We scrambled up. Mum had a wet mess of food and blood streaming down her face. Papa had thrown a full plate of food at her and hit her in the face. The metal plate caused a huge gash on her temple, just above the left eye. I screamed and started crying. Benny also started crying and ran towards Mum, grabbing onto her leg.

Papa yelled at us to shut up, or he would belt us. I glimpsed the familiar uncontrollable anger on his face and tried to stop the tears and snot streaming down my face.

Mum was trembling as she tried to wipe the mess from her face. "Get into the bedroom! Go!" she said to us.

"Why did you hit her?" Cecil screamed at Papa. He clenched his fists, pure hatred written all over his face. He was now fourteen and was on holiday from school. Papa whirled around and tried to grab him, but Cecil was too quick. He ducked and bolted outside, spilling the plates of food all over the floor, Papa hot on his heels.

"Kuki, call Rre Matona. Tell him that your father is out of control. Rami and Benny, get into the bedroom," Mum ordered.

Hyperventilating, I shouted, "No, Mum. We want to stay here!"

"Go!" Mum yelled, pointing towards Cecil's bedroom.

We stood by the bedroom door and refused to enter. The thought of Papa hurting Cecil terrified me. He often threatened to thrash him and throw him out of the house. He hated it when Cecil stood up to him for being violent to mum.

At moments like these, I hated Papa. I did not understand his behaviour. He made us all miserable.

Kuki ran across to call Rre Matona, who hurried back with her. He sat at the table opposite Mum. "Mma, what happened?" he asked.

Fighting back the tears, Mum responded, "*Rra.* I don't understand why Godfrey keeps doing this. I was asking him if my grandmother could come and stay for a few weeks. He got irritated. He refused and called her a troublemaker. I disagreed and pointed out that I tolerated his mother's visits. He lost his temper, and next thing I know, a plate of food landed on my face."

Before Rre Matona could respond, Papa, panting, came charging back in, a furious scowl on his face. "If Cecil talks to me like that again, I'll throw him out." He slammed his fist on the table, towering over mum. He ignored Rre Matona.

"*Dumela rra*," Rre Matona said to Papa.

Papa turned and looked at him. "*Dumela rra*. I'm sorry you had to come here again," Papa said.

"Well, Kuki came rushing to my house, distressed." Rre Matona looked at Kuki, who was standing beside him. He stood up and led her towards the bedroom door where Benny and I were standing. He smiled at us and ushered us in, reassuring us that all will be okay. He shut the door behind him.

We pinned our ears to the door, straining to hear what was being discussed. We could only hear muffled voices as Rre Matona talked to both my parents. I worried about Cecil and wanted him to come back home safe.

I overheard Mum say to Papa in a firm voice, "Godfrey, if that child does not come back to this house safe tonight, I'm going to report you to the police."

Papa's voice was inaudible and sounded subdued. Soon after, Rre Matona left to search for Cecil. He found him hiding in the bushes close by. He stayed in the house, talking to my parents for a little while longer, before leaving.

Mum came to us after Rre Matona left. She had some leftover food and urged us to eat it. We forced ourselves to eat. Papa had shut himself in the bedroom. That night mum slept with us on the dining room floor. Kuki had helped her clean up the mess before we set out our mats and blankets for sleeping. Mum refused to speak to Papa for days.

She stayed away from work, as her eyelid was black and swollen. The tension in the house was unbearable. You never knew what Papa would do. He was silent and kept to himself. He seemed sorry for what had happened.

A few days after the incident, Mum applied for leave and took us children with her to Lobatse to visit great-grandma for two weeks. We caught the overnight train to Lobatse. Papa's treatment of Cecil had disturbed Mum a lot, and I heard her talk to great-grandma Mma Motshitshi about it. Great-grandma told her she did not like the situation.

When we returned, Papa seemed relieved to have us back. He behaved much better, but I knew the peace was only temporary. I knew another fight would break out.

Even at that young age, I learned to read my parents' moods and tell from their voices or facial expression if trouble was on the horizon. I used this intuitive information to help prepare myself for the storm and tried to cope as best I could. The fights were frequent, with no long-term resolution.

I started trying to please Papa every day to make sure he relaxed, and the fights stopped. My own moods started being regulated by the moods of my parents. If I sensed any tension, I became miserable and tense, expecting a fight. I knew when Papa was brewing for a fight; he became quiet and moody. On such days I lost appetite and spent sleepless nights, not sure when conflict would erupt. The sense of anticipation of danger was debilitating.

We never discussed the subject of family violence. It was taboo. I developed a deep shame and embarrassment, as I knew people were aware of our family situation. On the outside, we were a model family, well known and well respected.

Whenever my siblings and I went into town, people would recognise us, "Hello, you are Godfrey's children. We know your father well. He's a wonderful man."

But behind closed doors, things were not right. Family violence was common in those days. Husbands assaulted their wives for whatever reason, and it was the accepted mode of discipline. Few men were keen to intervene in another's domestic issues. I suspect that even my father's relatives did not want to intervene too much in his private family matters.

Despite these tense times, there were lovely family moments. My parents exposed us to broad learning. They bought us books and music and took us to many places of interest, to expand our view of the world. Papa was a delight when he was in a jovial mood. He was very knowledgeable, and we did fun family things. He taught us to value the less fortunate and to help people where we could.

I remember him taking Kuki, Benny, and me to a music festival in Gaborone, where the latest popular South African bands were performing. He told us many stories of how he grew up, and we laughed and sang along the way. He was a different person when he was in a good mood. To me, Papa was a hero who knew everything. I loved him with all my heart.

My parents taught us the value of spirituality and believing in God. They were staunch Christians and attended church every Sunday. We all had to follow this routine. When I was little, I used to kneel and pray with Mum before going to bed.

Christianity alongside violence was another confusing contrast to me as a young child. The model parents I saw in church were not the ones I saw fighting.

I wished they would always stay as calm as they appeared when they were in church. Papa read the scripture most Sundays, which always made me proud. Mum belonged to the Saint Anna women's church movement. Every Sunday, she wore her Saint Anna church uniform, black skirt, white shirt, and a purple cape, with a black headscarf and black shoes. She clutched her bible under her arm as we all piled into the Vauxhall to drive to the Catholic mission for the ten o'clock mass.

The Saint Anna women made up the church choir and sang hymns in beautiful voices. I loved standing next to Mum and listening to her sing. I also loved the smell of her perfume. I buried my head in her clothes, often just to inhale her scent. After mass, we would hang around the church, waiting for Mum to finish her meetings.

CONTEXT AND REFLECTION

As a young girl facing a confusing life at home, I had no outlet. Mum dealt with her marital problems by withdrawing into herself and turning a blind eye to the impact on us.

Years later, she told me she had tried to seek help many times, but no one offered to help.

My sister Kuki became my primary support throughout this period of our lives. From a young age, she stepped in to become my rock. We had a special, tight, and unshakable bond that lasted until she passed on.

I knew the situation at home made her resentful, and many times she had big fights with Papa.

Chapter 5

A Different World

"For the lonely child who lacks comfort and understanding, to have pain means to feel wrong and bad. In this confusion of feeling bad with being bad, a tragic misunderstanding about the self takes root and begins to distort every aspect of life."

—Tom and Natalie Rusk

In late 1962 we moved from the African School to White City, another compound a few kilometres from the African School. The houses there were newer, with cleaner exterior paint and bigger, fenced yards. Our house had two bed-rooms, a living/dining room and a kitchen. The kitchen had a coal stove, a cupboard, and a sink.

The toilet was outside, to the rear of the house. It had a toilet seat and under the seat was a large metal bucket for sewage. The municipality collected the sewage every Monday morning around six. They used prisoners to collect and clean the buckets before bringing them back.

My friend Sentle, whom I met when we moved into the neighbourhood, warned me against using the toilet while the prisoners were removing the buckets. She said if they found me inside, they would open the door and smear poop on my face. I got stressed when sewage collection day arrived.

"Mum, what time are the prisoners coming to collect the bucket?" I asked one Monday morning.

"They come very early before you get out of bed. Why?"

"Sentle told me if they find me in the toilet, they will smear poop on my face."

"What rubbish. Don't listen to her."

Mum's words did not ease my fear of using the toilet without someone accompanying me. Apart from the prisoner situation, I was uncomfortable with the spiders and geckos high on the toilet wall. They made it hard to relax and poop in peace. I was always on the lookout. As soon as one moved, I bolted. As a result, I often avoided going to the toilet.

Our house faced a sports ground about five hundred metres away, where white people played rugby. I did not understand rugby. The ground looked like a soccer field with long goalposts at each end. Sometimes at night, there were bright, flickering lights on top of some posts.

"Look, ghosts!" Kuki yelled one night when we were out weeing on the dirt mound opposite our front gate.

"That's a lie. I'm going to tell Mum," I said, standing up without weeing. Ghosts scared the hell out of me.

"No, you are not," she said, poking me in the chest.

I shoved her away hard, and she tripped and fell. She got up and pushed me back.

"What did you do that for, fatso?" she said. I slapped her.

She grabbed my clothes and dragged me, and I started punching her hard on the head. I was taller and heavier than her and overpowered her.

Mum heard the commotion and came outside to separate us. "Stop! What is going on?" she asked.

"This fat baboon started hitting me for no reason," Kuki said.

"I am not a baboon. She often calls me fatso, and other names, and that's why I hit her!"

"Stop it, both of you. I told you not to fight!" Mum yelled as she ordered us back into the house. She removed her slipper and hit us hard on the backside.

This made me so mad! I planned revenge. I blamed Kuki for starting the fight. This was the normal pattern between us. We were close, but we fought like cat and mouse. She was prickly and had a fiery temper. Though she was much slimmer and shorter than me, she had quite a mouth on her. She teased me a lot and enjoyed taunting me about anything I did that she did not like.

I hated this. I often tried to walk away after many warnings for her to stop, but she carried on. In exasperation, I resorted to physical fights to get her to stop. She never won the fistfights, but she always won the war of words.

In 1963, my father left home to study at the university in Lesotho. That same year my second sister, Rose, arrived. She was a delightful, calm baby who never fussed about anything. She loved playing.

"How's the baby? Can we play with the baby?" The neighbours often asked.

I loved her and did not mind babysitting her. Mum was reluctant for neighbours to come and play with Rose. She said some neighbours were jealous and might harm her. Despite her misgiving, many neighbours and relatives came to visit to see the lovely baby they all adored.

Life in White City was more relaxed than at the African school. Mum was easier to be around, maybe because Papa was away. Papa and Cecil only came home during the holidays. We loved having them home. During this period, Mum and Papa were on much friendlier terms. There were occasional tensions, but they were not as frequent. As they say, absence makes the heart fonder.

Kuki and I had made new friends in the neighbourhood. Our closest friends were Sentle, Mmapula, and Noni, who lived next door behind our house. We used to play hide and seek outside at night in the bright moonlight, wearing dark clothes to conceal ourselves. We avoided the neighbours on the right side of our house. The man, Mr Nongo, was weird and used to call me his wife, which I detested.

Sometimes Mum's relatives from Lobatse came to stay. They helped Mum to look after us. Great-grandma Mma Motshitshi came to visit often. She loved the local brew and visited the locations to drink. She often came home sloshed, much to our delight and Mum's annoyance.

Sometimes she brought the local mophane worms to fry and snack on. Street vendors boil and salt the worms before drying them in the sun. They are a popular savoury delicacy in Botswana. They have a distinct pungent aroma and are an acquired taste. Mum couldn't stomach them and forbade great-grandma to share them with us. I hated them anyway. I tried them once and got sick. I used to sit fascinated watching great-grandma grab a fat worm, throw it into her mouth and chew away, head and all.

"Great-grandma, why don't you cut the head and bum off?" I would ask.

"Those are the best bits," she would respond with a laugh, slurring her words.

Great-grandma often stayed with us for months at a time. She was quiet when sober, but her inhibitions flew out the window when drunk. She swore at anyone and everyone in the neighbourhood.

Mum disliked swearing and forbade anyone to swear around us. Whenever Mum tried to stop her, great-grandma reeled off one profanity after another, sometimes at us, which was hilarious.

"I told you not to swear in front of the children, and you ignored me," Mum said one morning after a drunk, bad swearing episode.

"I don't remember. I played with Rami and Benny, but I don't remember swearing at them," Great-grandma said. You could tell by her sly look that she remembered it well.

"Oh, yes, you did. You are just denying it." Mum ended up not talking to her for days. It got lonely whenever great-grandma travelled back home to Lobatse. She was fun to have around.

One morning, when Papa was home for the holidays, he and Mum went shopping. Rose spotted them walking back home from afar and pointed. We ran towards them, expecting sweets and treats. When they got closer to us, we realised Papa was carrying a small, shiny, and compact case. Both our parents were beaming.

"Papa, what is that?" Benny asked, pointing to the briefcase.

"It's a gramophone," Papa said with pride. "Let's go inside. I'll show you what it does."

We all followed him into the small dining room. He placed the shiny brand-new gold gramophone on the table. Mum was carrying four vinyl LP records by Jim Reeves, The Beatles, the Kings Messengers Quartet, and Virginia Lee. They had bought the gramophone and records from J. Haskins and sons, one of the largest shops in town. Africans were now allowed to shop in town and live in previously segregated areas.

We were so excited! This was different from the small, grey, and hissy radio that blasted news and music daily from the dining-room windowsill. We gathered around in excitement as Papa connected a large, brick-like blue battery to the back of the gramophone.

He opened the gramophone lid, took the King's Messengers Quartet record from the table where Mum had placed the records, and tore the plastic covering off. We were like hawks, jostling for the best view, as he placed the record on the gramophone and lowered the stylus onto the disk. Magic! The sweetest harmonious voices filled the entire house, a perfect mixture of soprano alto, contralto, and bass.

"Papa, who are they? They sing so well," Kuki asked.

"They are a Christian gospel group from South Africa," he said.

I grabbed the cover, staring at the picture of four well-groomed and smartly dressed African men. Their grey suits were impeccable. They stood next to each other; bright eyes cast upwards to the heavens, focusing on a brilliant white light. They all had short, cropped hair, and one had a trimmed beard. The cover was smooth to the touch and smelled new.

"Give it over to me," Benny tried to grab the cover off me.

I lifted my hand out of reach, refusing to give it to him. He started crying.

"Give it to him," Mum scolded.

I gave the cover over to Benny. He passed it around, with everyone taking turns to touch and sniff it.

Next, we listened to the Beatles. Kuki fell head over heels in love with Paul McCartney. I liked John. Our preferences led to a nasty argument over whether Paul was better looking than John.

In the beginning, we could not play the gramophone ourselves. We had to ask Papa or Mum to play it for us. After a few weeks, once we had got the hang of it, Papa allowed us to play it.

"Be careful not to drop the stylus on it! You'll scratch the record," I said to Kuki as she changed the record.

"I'm careful, and I know we should not scratch it. Why don't you leave me alone? I know what I'm doing!" she turned towards me, irritated.

Kuki and I often fought each other to play our favourite music. We raced home after school, seeing who could eat fastest, and be the one to turn the gramophone on.

That little gold gramophone brought us considerable pleasure for many years. A few years later, my parents bought a bigger, more sophisticated, and powerful gramophone with an inbuilt space to store records.

We bought records with our pocket money and listened to music from all over the world. Music provided solace for us and created a light mood in the house. My siblings and I liked to sit together in the dining room after lunch, listening and singing along to our favourite music. Sometimes we would read while listening to music.

To this day, I remember those days with much fondness. Such moments brought me peace, despite my internal insecurities and fears.

STARTING SCHOOL

That same year, at six years old, I started primary school and joined Kuki at the local Our Lady of the Desert Catholic school. It was a school for African children only. Mixed-race schools didn't exist at that time.

The school was next to the church that we attended every Sunday, and I was familiar with it. I knew most of the sisters and priests from church. I felt shy and uncomfortable when they spoke to me. All I could manage was "Yes, Sister," or "Yes, Father," as I ducked behind my mother's skirt at the earliest opportunity. The principal of the school was Bishop Murphy, a big, burly, and chirpy Irish priest. He used to play with Benny and me, pinching our cheeks and pulling our ears. I was shy and terrified of him.

I loathed some classes and the style of teaching. Teachers emphasised rote learning. They punished us if we gave wrong answers, were late for class, or talked during class. Punishment included pinching, beating with a stick, or rapping the knuckles with a ruler. The teachers shamed and belittled us in front of the class, which was stressful and humiliating. Some teachers were just plain sadistic.

I remember when Benny started school; he shared a distressing incident of his maths class teacher, whom they had nicknamed Mopo because he was cross-eyed. Mopo asked the boys a question and did not specify who he was talking to. Instead, he nodded his head toward the direction of a group of boys.

"You boy, what's seven times seven?" he asked. He realised the boys were unsure who he was referring to, as he didn't appear to focus his eyes on one boy in particular.

"Stand up!" he barked. The boys looked around in confusion. Four boys, Benny included, shot up. He marched towards them and slapped Benny and two other boys.

"Who asked you to stand up? Sit down and shut up! You, answer the question." He now pointed to the fourth boy. The other boys sat down, upset. Mopo seemed to derive perverse pleasure from torturing the poor boys. Such incidents of teachers punishing students for no valid reason were very common and occurred daily.

I found it difficult to adjust to school life. Some students were pretty heartless and enjoyed starting fights daily and dominating others.

"There's a fight at the school gate after class; who is coming?" someone announced in class. As soon as the end-of-day school bell rang, a large group of kids gathered like a pack of hungry wolves at the school gates. They threw their bags on the ground, jostling for the best viewing position and baying for blood. Monaka, the perpetrator, appointed herself referee.

She scooped soil from the ground and instructed the fighters, "Here, slap this off my hand," and they both obliged. This signalled that each opponent accepted the challenge and was ready to fight.

Fists, slaps, and kicks flew amidst the deafening shouts until one kid dropped to the ground, bleeding from the nose. "Get up, you coward!" school kids screamed at her.

The fight stopped when a teacher approached, sending the group scattering in all directions like flies. The kid who lost became the butt of cruel, shaming jokes and ridicule for weeks afterwards. Such incidents happened on a regular basis.

Sometimes I got dragged into the fights. They were humiliating and stressful, and they worsened my fragile and vulnerable state. I always ended up in tears, alone, and lost. The helplessness I sometimes experienced at home extended to school.

Whenever I tried to stick up for myself, I ended up being shamed and assaulted. The one skill that I had learned well was to read other people's moods and adjust my actions to please them, to avoid any confrontation. This ability came in handy many times. I shared my sweets and treats with the bullies to get them off my back.

I was a tomboy by nature and loved to question and explore things. Papa instilled in me a curiosity for learning and questioning new things. This provided a great escape and mental stimulus for me. It also got me into trouble often.

Rigid, unrealistic rules and expectations bored me. That trait landed me in trouble with my peers and teachers. They misinterpreted it for arrogance, and I was often falsely accused of thinking that the other students were not as clever as I. I did well in school, receiving straight-As, and excelled at English, history, science, and mathematics. I was always top of the class. That made me even more unpopular. I know many kids viewed Kuki and me as privileged and resented us for that.

Despite the difficulties, I had fantastic friends at school. My two best friends, Setso and Sentle, were my classmates. They were my age, and we got on well. We had lots of fun and adventure. We tried to stay away from the school bullies as much as we could.

The three of us often disappeared into the surrounding bushes during the school break to forage for wild berries away from other students. We shared our food during meal breaks and enjoyed telling entertaining stories.

Setso lived in the eastern part of town, in a rambling old British colonial home, with a large orchard with many fruit trees. She often brought juicy mandarins or prickly pears to share, depending on what was in season.

We loved playing together after school and did not go home until late in the afternoon. We enjoyed playing skipping rope in the middle of the road, often jumping off just in time for some old truck or donkey-driven scotch cart to go past, covering us with dust. Scotch carts were two-wheeled carts drawn by donkeys or oxen. They were a popular and affordable mode of transportation for the local Africans.

Sometimes we played a hop, step, and jump game, which involved drawing squares on the road and jumping over them in a pattern. There was never a sense of competition between us. We just enjoyed each other's company and had few fights.

I loved the red soil around the school and on the way home. It stretched for miles. The area was dotted with bushes and shrubs and different sized anthills from which rows and rows of black ants appeared and disappeared all day long. "Let's go eat the soil from the anthill," Sentle would say. "My sister said the soil is good to eat. Just be careful of ant bites."

I refused to partake. I had tried it once. There was a live ant stuck to it, which I crunched on. The ant tasted unpleasant and tart. I also hated the crunch of soil on my teeth. The area also had many cactus plants, some of which had sweet prickly fruit that we loved picking. We had to be careful of sharp thorns.

The trip from school to home was rich with adventure. There was plenty to do. When it rained, we followed Kuki and her friends to the river for a swim. The river only flowed when heavy rains came, which was rare, given Botswana's arid environment.

It was exciting when the river was flowing. Lots of kids trekked straight to the river after school. We placed school uniforms and books under the trees away from the water as we stripped to our knee-length bloomers and plunged into the cold, muddy brown water.

Most of us could not swim. We just waded into the murky water and splashed about, sometimes diving in. Afterwards, we dressed and wandered home, ensuring that our parents did not know we had been in the water.

The water was quite dangerous after heavy rain; it was hard to gauge how fast the undercurrent was.

One day after we returned home from swimming, two police officers arrived at our house, inquiring about Setso's whereabouts. Mum called us out of the bedroom. "Were you girls with Setso today after school?" she asked.

"Yes, we parted ways after playing," I said, scared and apprehensive. *Why were the police here, looking for Setso?* I thought.

"Did you girls go swimming?" Mum asked, looking at both of us.

"No, Mum," Kuki and I lied.

One officer addressed us. "Setso did not go home after school. Her father has searched all over for her and can't find her," he said. Then he continued, "Two girls drowned this afternoon swimming. Are you girls sure you did not go swimming with Setso?"

"No, sir," Kuki replied. "We parted ways after playing, and she continued home as usual."

The police left shortly after, assuring Mum that they would keep her updated with Setso's situation. The news of the drowning spooked me, and I worried about Setso, but I was sure she had not gone back to the river when we parted ways. Like me, she feared getting into the water by herself.

I shivered and wished they would find her safe. Mum gave us a stern lecture about swimming in the river. I could tell the news of missing girls had distressed her.

Later in the evening, a neighbour informed Mum that Setso was okay and at home. The explanation she gave to her father was that she played with her dolls under the dining table when she got home. She was tired and fell asleep. No one searched for her there. She did not mention going swimming, which was a relief!

I did not sleep much that night. News of the drowning traumatised me. I had never confronted death before. The following day during school assembly, the principal announced that the two students who had drowned were eight-year-old Elizabeth Smarts and her six-year-old younger sister.

Francistown was small in those days, and many people in the township knew each other. The entire school community attended their funeral the following week.

Their mother's tortured wail pierced the air as a group of men used ropes to lower their white, wooden coffins into the ground, next to each other. That picture stayed vivid in my mind for years. I never swam in the river again.

MAHALAPYE

When Papa completed university in 1966, the government posted him to Mahalapye to work as Education Officer, looking after schools in the Central district. He took over from a white man. We moved into a white neighbourhood.

Our house was a beautiful post-colonial three-bedroomed house with electricity and running water. The house had a well-established garden with grapes, banana, peach, and citrus trees. We had a vegetable patch growing carrots and spinach. The chicken coop at the corner of the yard housed about ten chickens.

Our house was at the corner of a wide street, and our neighbours to the right were Mr and Mrs Meskim, a middle-aged, friendly British couple. Mr Meskim's skin was sunburned, with many dark sunspots on his large hairy arms and head. He liked to play with us. Whenever he saw us, he would come running towards us, his face beaming and shouting with a booming voice, "*Siya, siya*, run, run." Benny, Rose, and I would scatter around squealing with a mixture of fear and laughter, not wanting him to catch us.

Mrs Meskim came around to our house a lot, always bringing some yummy cake she had baked. She had flawless, porcelain skin and a beautiful smile. I loved watching her and Mum have a cup of tea together on the veranda. Mum was pregnant with my sister Nelly, who was born in August of that year.

I remember Mrs Meskim coming to the house, impeccable in a bright green and yellow floral dress, excited to see the baby. Her high heels tapped on the red, polished cement floor as she made her way to Mum's bedroom, where Nelly lay on a white cot. She lifted her into her arms, beaming and rocking her. I stood at the door, gazing at her. She was so pretty.

Besides the Meskims, the local Catholic priest used to bring us fresh vegetables every week. Mum always baked a cake for the priests and took it to the mission when we went to church on Sunday.

Life in Mahalapye was great and relaxed. Papa sold the Vauxhall and bought a brand-new Chevrolet truck and used it to take us on holidays to many places across Botswana. We visited and explored the surrounding villages and some-times travelled to Gaborone or Lobatse to visit relatives. During school holidays, we accompanied him on his school inspection trips around the district. We also went on trips to visit my maternal grandmother in Bobonong, the village where Papa was born.

One time, Papa took Benny and me with him to visit her. We left Mahalapye very early in the morning. It had rained the previous night. The road was muddy and slippery. About two hours into the trip, we came to the river Lebetu. It was a medium-sized river, and sometimes if the river was full, vehicles got bogged or swept away.

This morning, the river was swollen, and the water was swift, dragging lots of debris as it flowed. There was no bridge. A few cars and scotch carts had stopped on either side of the river; it was too dangerous to cross. A man came over when our Chevrolet truck pulled up.

"*Dumela rra,*" he said to Papa.

"*Dumela rra.* How long has the river been flowing?" Papa asked.

"It's been like this since yesterday evening. The water is starting to subside."

"Is the crossing deep here?"

"It can be. However, you should be able to manage with your big truck."

Papa hesitated. We got out of the truck and walked towards the flowing river. Large, overhanging trees lined the banks of the river, making it look quite dangerous. The hissing sound of the swift current was menacing. Papa decided we should wait for a few hours before attempting to cross. He sat and chatted with the men. Benny and I played nearby.

After a few hours, Papa decided the water had subsided enough—it was time to go. It was a nerve-wracking moment when he eased the Chevrolet into the river. He shifted gears as he navigated his way to the opposite bank. The truck strained and revved noisily as we inched closer to the bank. Benny and I held onto the dashboard, excited but scared at the same time.

"Are we going to manage, Papa?" Benny asked.

"Yes, we will. Just hold on tight."

We crossed the river amid loud cheers from the spectators. Papa's Chevrolet was a big, robust, and imposing truck, which could tackle turbulent currents. The vehicle was for off-road, rough terrain, and Papa loved putting it through its paces. After crossing, he parked the truck and walked back toward the riverbank to watch other drivers attempt the crossing. He was ready in case a vehicle needed to be pulled out of the water. He always carried strong ropes in the truck for such occasions. Fortunately, all those we watched made it without needing help.

We left soon after and continued our trip to Bobonong. There were few settlements along the route we took. Most dwellings were cattle posts, spaced miles from each other. The few people we saw were either herdsmen or hunters, looking to kill game. The area had lots of ostriches, deer, and wildebeests. Deer and wildebeest meat were delicacies and highly sought after. Local people hunted them and shared the meat with neighbours and relatives.

We arrived in Bobonong in the late afternoon. Grandmother and my aunts were excited to see us, as they'd heard reports that the Lebetu River was full. Grandmother chastised Papa for taking the risk to cross the raging river. You could tell she was relieved he was alright.

Soon many relatives arrived at grandmother's compound, as word had gone around that Papa was in Bobonong. The atmosphere was lively as people sat around the fire, sharing food and relating stories of adventure and catching up with Papa. We stayed in Bobonong for a few days, visiting relatives before driving back to Mahalapye. By the time we returned, the river was almost dry.

I loved these trips to visit our relatives. Some of them travelled from the surrounding villages to see us. They all loved Papa very much and gave us a warm welcome. I wished we could visit more often, but Mum was not too keen.

A few years later, Papa changed jobs again, and we moved back to Francistown in 1969. Kuki and I were in our last year in primary school. I was twelve.

CONTEXT AND REFLECTION

Harmonious family moments were very good and enjoyable. I loved these moments of peace in the household and was happy when there was no tension. I loathed confrontation in any situation.

I struggled emotionally with school, and a part of me felt lonely and sad. I lived with a heightened sense of anticipated danger.

Chapter 6

Where the Fittest Prevail

"When the child within feels unsafe, it creates a lot of trouble."

—*Louise Hay*

The year was 1970. Kuki and I had finished primary school and were waiting for high school admission. We had performed extremely well in our primary school exams and had applied to a couple of Catholic schools. The daily anxiety of not knowing if we had made it to high school was torture.

Kuki and I shared the same class from grade four when I caught up with her; she had struggled in her early schooling years and had to repeat some grades.

One morning, Mum went into town to check mail for the umpteenth time as she did almost daily. We heard her car arrive in front of the house, and the usual anticipation took over. I said a silent prayer. Mum's little red Volkswagen, which she bought when we returned to Francistown, came to a hasty stop in front of the garage. She leapt out, brandishing a large brown, bulky envelope and a piece of white paper in the air.

Kuki and I dashed towards her in anticipation, stumbling over each other, eyes glued on the paper.

"Come and have a look at this," she said. Her glowing face could not contain her excitement. She thrust the sheet of paper towards us, exposing a pretty, sketched sky blue, school tunic with a broad belt. She had our complete attention.

"Lovely! Who is it for?" I asked, clasping the paper.

"It's for both of you. It's a picture of your school uniform." Mum inched closer, handing the sheet to me. "You are going to St Joseph's College," she said.

"Yippee, how marvellous. When do we leave?" I danced around the backyard as Kuki snatched the paper from my hand.

The commotion and excitement had attracted Rose, Benny, and Nelly. They came outside, watching on with eager interest. "You leave next month. We need to get you ready," she responded.

"Oh, my God, that's so close!" Kuki shrieked as her eyes cast back at the paper, almost caressing the picture of the uniform.

"Show me," Nelly stuck out her little palm, trying to snatch the paper from Kuki's hand.

"Careful, Nelly. Don't damage it," Mum said.

Kuki handed the sheet to Nelly. Rose and Benny leaned in for a closer view. Mum pulled out another piece of paper from the envelope. The form had a lengthy list of items the college wanted us to bring. They included nightclothes, cardigans, socks, shirts and skirts, bedsheets and blankets, right down to the undergarment and how much pocket money we were to have. We were each allowed one suitcase or clothes chest.

St Joseph's College was one of the most prestigious high schools in Botswana. It was a Catholic-run boarding school reputed for providing the highest quality education. It was rare for my parents to praise me, but on this day, Mum radiated pride and approval. I realised why Mum was so thrilled. Education, for the local community, was critical to secure a bright future.

"Come on, hand the papers back. Kuki and Rami, we have to review this list later and plan shopping." Mum put everything back into the envelope.

We couldn't wait to share the wonderful news with Papa. That night, we had a special treat. Dinner included pudding to celebrate Kuki and my final primary school exam achievement.

Two days after we received our admission letters, Kuki and I were tidying the kitchen when Mum wandered in. She sat down at the small, wooden kitchen table, a pensive expression on her face. We sensed something was wrong, so we stopped and came over to join her.

"You girls will meet students from different households and traditions at college. You need to protect yourselves and be vigilant," she said.

"Yes, Mum." We said in unison, baffled.

"Many of their families practice witchcraft."

I could sense tension building and peeked at Kuki, who looked frustrated. These conversations peeved her. She did not believe in witchcraft and made her views clear to Mum at every opportunity, which often ended in conflict. I fence-sat on the subject and erred on the side of caution by supporting the protection argument. I did not wish to displease Mum.

"Here you go again, Mum; I don't want to get embroiled in any of this cleansing business. You know that." Kuki said.

Mum stiffened, looking daggers at Kuki. "Listen, don't start that rubbish. This is serious. I know what I am doing. How dare you question my decision!"

Kuki shot back. "This stuff is not true. I know you want us to visit faith healers. They're a waste of money. I won't go!"

"Don't you talk to me like that. You will do as I say. And that's that." Mum stormed out of the kitchen, almost knocking the chair over.

Dead silence. I stole another peek at Kuki. She was livid. *Better leave this one alone*, I thought to myself. I had learned not to buy into Kuki's arguments with Mum on this topic. I always ended up getting caught in the crossfire.

Many African cultures believe in witchcraft and evil spirits. People spend much time and money fighting this scourge. They visit witch doctors, traditional healers, spiritual or faith healers to protect themselves. The spiritual and faith healers are like sages, energy healers, Reiki masters, and shamans in other cultures. People respect them a lot.

Mum preferred spiritual and faith healers. She visited them to seek help through any challenges in her life, be it our schooling, her job, and our general health and well-being. She believed these faith healers could undo or prevent any witchcraft or ill will, which she alleged envious people used to damage others' lives or kill them.

Mum imposed her belief in the powers of faith healers on us. Any refusal to conform to her wishes to visit the healers for cleansing brought out her wrath. Her confidence in their abilities to protect herself and us from evil was unshakeable.

Many spiritual healers had their own large churches that local people attended. People travelled to them to undergo prayer healing, cleansing baths fortified with special solutions and potions, and secret healing ceremonies conducted in the dark of night. Some churches followed clandestine practices steeped in mysticism, and others carried out ritualistic sacrifices. Some asked devotees to sacrifice their children. Mum avoided those like the plague.

Before we left for college, we visited Mma Omponye. She was a powerful and popular faith healer and had a church in Monarch, a riverside location a few kilometres from our home.

Her church compound was expansive. We could see the blue wooden front entrance of the church facing the main gate as we approached. Amid a spacious, wire fenced dusty courtyard, grass-thatched mud huts and small brick houses surrounded the church. Some dwellings housed deacons, attendants, and other church members who lived in the compound. Other rooms and huts were used for healing and cleansing people.

Blue and white were the congregation's uniform colours, and the place was a hive of bustling colour as we arrived. The evening service had finished, and members of the congregation stayed back for cleansing. People shuffled backward and forward from the cleansing rooms, hauling buckets of water to run healing baths.

Ishmael, a deacon, led us into the church where Mma Omponye sat on a high chair at an altar lit by many flickering and glowing candles. She looked imposing in her blue and white striped robe and blue sash, held in place by a knotted white woven rope secured around her ample midriff. A white headscarf covered her head. You could glimpse a few tufts of grey hair under the scarf. On the floor next to her lay a long sceptre, draped in the blue and white church colours.

She appeared regal and imposing, an image of spiritual authority and mystery that somehow reassured me we were in expert hands. Church women sat on the floor close by. Mma Omponye was sitting in silent meditation when the deacon ushered us in. She opened her thick arms to embrace us as we moved towards her, Mum pushed us from behind. She enveloped us in an affectionate hug. I liked the slight whiff of camphor and burning incense around her.

"Welcome, my children. You girls are about to go off to high school, I gather. Such wonderful news," she said. "Congratulations, Mma," she said to Mum, who beamed back in appreciation.

Clearly, Mum had seen her earlier and told her the news. Ishmael asked us to wait outside the church while Mma Omponye and Mum talked.

"I detest these events," Kuki said as we waited.

"They are not all dreadful, you know. I like Mma Omponye. At least she's charming and seems to know what she's doing." I was careful with my words to avoid a clash.

Kuki sighed in resignation. "They're all the same. Anyway, I hope we're not here all night. I wish Papa were home."

True. Mum only took us to these places when Papa was not home. Papa thought she wasted a lot of money on these practices.

Mma Omponye emerged from the church a little while later, followed by Mum. She invited us to follow her. We all filed behind her as she led us along a narrow, moonlit footpath towards the river, a short distance from the church compound. The night sky was alive with a multitude of stars. She walked with a noticeable limp, dawdling her bulky body along, her heavy breath smoking in the chilly night air. She carried her sceptre in one hand and a small metal pail with miscellaneous paraphernalia in the other.

The night was quiet, except for our shoes crunching on the rocky gravel. Dogs barked as we trudged past mud huts lit by flickering candlelight. The vast moonlit white sand captivated us as we left the houses behind and meandered through short shrubs towards the river. The scene was hypnotic. Mma Omponye led us to a secluded area along the bank. She signalled us to stop at an area that looked set for a ceremony. There was a full bucket of water sitting there. We stood by, awaiting further instruction. Mma Omponye went to stand next to the bucket and turned towards Kuki.

"You, older girl, take off all your clothes and come and squat over here and face that direction," she pointed east with her sceptre. Kuki hesitated and then started stripping, looking resentful.

"You, young lady," she turned towards me, "take off your clothes as well, and follow me." I took my clothes off and gave them to Mum to hold. I was nervous. *I wonder what she's going to do!*

Kuki moved to her designated spot. I followed Mma Omponye to where another bucket full of water was already waiting; no doubt placed there earlier by her deacons. She retrieved what looked like a packet of ash from the small bucket, splashed some contents into the water, chanting prayers as she swirled the liquid around the bucket.

"Squat here and face that direction." I obeyed.

She held the top of my head with her hand as she bent to scoop water with the other. An icy blast of water hit my back. I gasped, struggling to stand up. I fought hard not to let out a fart; I would die of embarrassment if I let one rip! She clasped me down in place, her prayer recitals now a constant, hypnotic chant.

I sensed she was reciting verses from the bible, but I could not concentrate on the prayers. She bent down again and this time used the small metal pail to scoop the water. A cold, steady trickle flowed over my head as she rubbed my hair and face, chanting under her breath. I couldn't breathe and tried to brush her hand off.

"Stand up," she instructed.

Thank God! She bent and scooped more water, and this time poured it on my torso as she rubbed and chanted. After the initial violent shiver from the icy cold water, my body felt warm. She kept scooping water into the small bucket until all the water finished. She tapped my shoulders and head with the sceptre and made a sign of the cross across my forehead with ointment. She concluded by reciting the Lord's prayer.

"Alright, we're done. Dry yourself off with this cloth and go put your clothes back on." She pulled a cloth from a pocket in her robe and ambled towards where Kuki was waiting. What a relief it was over! I chuckled to myself as I hurried back towards Mum, imagining the icy, brutally cold water on Kuki's naked, skinny backside. She was going to hate it! I wished I could be there to witness her reaction! I was so right.

Kuki emerged a short while later, stomping towards us, shivering, shell-shocked, and pissed off. Her fury made her slim body stiff and even smaller. I stuck a fist in my mouth, biting hard on my knuckles to stop the laughter. I knew I would never live that one down! She could cut me to size with a few select words. She glared at Mum without uttering a word. Mum kept her mouth shut, no doubt praying that Kuki say nothing out loud to embarrass her.

We walked back to the church compound in silence and stayed for a little while longer before saying our goodbyes. Kuki was civil enough in her goodbyes, though she avoided eye contact with everyone.

It must have been midnight when we drove back home. You could have sliced the tension in the car with a knife. I prayed that Kuki and Mum don't start one of their epic fights. They were like a dog with a bone. Once they started, they did not stop. Their fights were exhausting and affected everyone in the house for days.

When we arrived home, Kuki flung the car door open and charged out, slamming it behind her. Mum clicked her tongue in anger but did not say much.

"Get to bed," she ordered me. *Yeah, take it out on me!*

I obliged. I hurried to our bedroom, where my younger sisters were already fast asleep. Kuki was already there, getting ready for bed, fumes of rage still billowing from her ears. I changed into my nightie and jumped into bed, avoiding talking to her. *No dumping on me this time!*

I never questioned the truth or lack thereof of the faith-healing practices. I did not mind them unless the places we visited were dirty and the people rude.

Unlike my sister Kuki, I also know that I gave in to avoid the fights with Mum. Kuki's mettle and determination to fight for her rights was something I admired very much. I didn't have the guts.

We spent the days leading up to our departure shopping and preparing for the long journey. Papa was now back home from his work trips.

We departed Francistown on a sunny Sunday morning in January 1970 and boarded the overnight train to Kgale Siding, where St Joseph's College was. We each had a brand-new black trunk packed full of clothes and toiletries. We had a small basket with provisions. Kuki had cooked chicken and baked rock buns for us to take. My parents and my younger siblings, Benny, Rose, and Nelly, came to the station to say goodbye. Cecil was away at University in Lesotho.

Papa carried our luggage into the sleeper compartment and helped us settle in. He encouraged us to find other students who were also going to St Joseph's. My parents were sombre and worried.

The train whistle blew, and soon the long, steam train ambled out of the station. I fought back tears as we waved goodbye—this was the first time I was leaving home, and I was petrified. I was a few weeks shy of my thirteenth birthday.

ARRIVING IN KGALE

The train horn honked at around three a.m. and within minutes pulled into Kgale Siding. The night was dark; the siding was not lit. St Joseph's was located in a rural area a few kilometres from Gaborone. We could glimpse the dim lights of the college in the distance, in between large trees and shrubs.

We were ready. We had woken up an hour earlier to wash and get dressed.

The arrival scene was almost comical as hundreds of boys and girls disembarked, shouting greetings and instructions at each other. Chaos ensued as people threw trunks, suitcases, and blankets from train windows and train doorways before jumping off, some through the windows—people had forewarned us that the train stopped for only ten minutes.

We alighted and stood on the gravel away from the train, watching the commotion. My eyes bulged as I tried to make sense of my surroundings.

Then I heard a loud voice coming towards us. "Welcome, *mesela*," a derogatory greeting to us newbies. Three big, mean-looking girls approached us.

"Hey *mosela*, where are you from?" one girl asked Kuki.

"I'm from Francis..." the girl shoved her fingers on Kuki's face before she could finish her answer. How rude! Kuki recoiled in shock.

"C'mon, *mosela*. Carry my trunk." The girl pointed to a large trunk further back on the ground.

"I have my own trunk to carry," Kuki said.

"What? Who are you talking to like that?" Another shoved her face.

I wanted to intervene to defend my sister, but the big girls scared me.

"Pick up that trunk," the girl barked at her, with her mates standing by, watching. Kuki relented.

The train had left, leaving us in the dark, except for torchlight carried by students.

Kuki and another new girl struggled to pick up the heavy trunk and disappeared into the darkness along the narrow, rough path towards the school dormitories. The entire scene was eerie and surreal. I stood riveted to my spot, not wanting Kuki to leave me with these strangers, but I had to stay back to watch our luggage.

I was lucky that some girls we had shared the carriage with stayed back with me. This frenzied torture of new students was all around us. Some older students resembled wild animals baying for fresh blood. They subjected us, new students, to the humiliating treatment of shoving fingers on our faces as if it were some initiation ritual. I had to close my eyes to avoid them getting poked and injured.

We made our way from the siding, dragging our trunks in the dark. The noise of many trunks being lugged was deafening, upsetting, and ominous. I sensed tough times ahead.

St Joseph's was a boarding college for boys and girls. It was run by Irish Jesuit priests and nuns. A gravel road passed in the middle of the school, leading to the teacher's quarters on the northern side. The road served as a boundary segregating the boys' and girls' lodging quarters. The girls' dormitories were located on the eastern side of the road and had dedicated accommodation for junior and senior school year students.

Kuki and I were allocated to Dormitory One, one of two old dormitories for new students. We had to climb five big concrete stairs to get into the barely lit, drab, long hall, with a grey concrete floor.

Ten single metal beds lined each side of the hall. Each bed had a dirty, sagging sisal mattress and no pillow. Next to each bed stood a wide-open, tall, and empty grey metal clothes locker. I imagined prison cells to look like this. Each dormitory had a prefect, responsible for ensuring the room was orderly and informing us of the dormitory rules. Our prefect was a Form Three student, Mpho. She was older than me, the same age as Kuki.

"There are no adjacent beds," I muttered to Kuki, close to tears.

"I know. Look, there's a spare bed in that corner, close to the wall. You take that one, and I'll take the one closer to the door."

I looked around the room. The misery was palpable all around. Most girls were sitting upon their beds, looking scared, and some cried. Kuki and I walked towards the bed I was to occupy. It was next to a small darkish looking girl who was sitting on her already made-up bed, wiping away tears. She stopped crying and sat staring at us, her eyes following us around the room as Kuki helped me unpack my trunk.

What could I say to her? Welcome to paradise. We both understood the hellish situation that was unfolding around us. I felt sorry for her. At least I had my older sister with me. Older students from other dormitories kept streaming in and out, shouting obscenities and calling us *mesela* as we were trying to settle in.

After changing into our nighties, Kuki and I walked outside to the wash hall to brush our teeth. The wash hall was about twenty meters away from the dormitory, accessed by climbing more concrete stairs.

The room was dingy, with dirty grey interior walls. Ten concrete washbasins, each with a cold-water tap, lined the wall's length, and behind them were ten toilet cubicles, a few with broken doors. We brushed our teeth in a hurry, careful not to drop our shiny new toothbrushes in the dirty sinks, and returned to the dormitory to sleep.

My sleep was fitful, and I kept waking up. The bed was uncomfortable, and the room was eerie and full of strange shadows. The sound of owls from the surrounding large trees made me think of ghosts. Ding dong, ding dong—the sound of a bell persisted in the background as I tried to sleep. *We have only just gone to bed!* I thought. It was five in the morning.

"Everyone get up. Bathing time," the prefect shouted.

Girls jumped out of bed, grabbed whatever wash toiletries they had, and rushed outside to the wash hall. I was still sleepy and slow. I changed into my beautiful pink new gown and grabbed my washing cloth, soap, and toothbrush, and walked towards the wash hall, barefoot.

A stunning sight greeted me as I walked in. Naked girls of all shapes and sizes, talking in animation to each other, were at the washbasins, scooping cold water with their hands and throwing it on their backs. Some girls were scrubbing their feet on old pumice stones. There was no pretence at modesty.

Dirty and frothy pinkish looking water, which was not draining, flowed all over the floor towards us as we lined up, awaiting our turn to bathe. The stench of sewage was overpowering, and I tried not to gag. I did not understand why the water was pink. A few days later, I learned why, as some girls talked in hushed tones about their periods, a subject unfamiliar to me.

As the first group of girls finished bathing, it was our turn to step into the disgusting, watery mess to wash. I had hoped the floor would get flushed before we washed—no such luck. We waded barefoot into the filth to find a free basin. My washbasin was slimy, and the water was freezing cold. I washed as best as I could, careful not to drop my toiletries into the water.

After the wash, I rushed to the dormitory and dressed in my new uniform. The prefect had informed us that there was to be a cleaning roster. I prayed to God that I did not get rostered to the wash hall. Eventually, I did, as we all had to take turns.

The breakfast bell rang, and several of us walked together to the dining hall. The hall was a swarm of activity, packed with boys and girls sitting at large metal tables, eating a measly breakfast from tin plates. They stared at us as we walked in but dared not insult us as the Matron and the Boarding Master were in the hall, supervising.

The Matron looked after all the girls, and the Boarding master was responsible for the boys. A Head Girl and Head Boy assisted them, and they had several prefects under them. I made sure I sat next to Kuki and ate as much of my porridge as I could. I was starving. Breakfast was an unappealing plate of cold porridge with milk and sugar, a thin slice of bread with jam, and a tin mug filled with weak coffee. I was really missing home.

Ding dong—the bell rang before we could finish our food. I scoffed as much down as I could and followed everyone towards a courtyard where the principal, Father John, stood on a podium, waiting to begin assembly.

He was a tall and striking priest. He wore a long black habit, with a large Jesuit cross hanging from his neck, giving him a distinct authoritarian look. On his right were nuns in grey and white and a large team of mixed-race teachers, including the Matron and Boarding Master. Rows of students in sky blue and grey uniforms stood in silence in front of the podium where he was standing.

He started assembly. "First of all, welcome to the new students," he said. He opened the red bible he was carrying and read scripture, then the whole assembly recited the Lord's prayer. Father John spelled out the school regulations and explained the order of the school day. He called the Head Girl and Head Boy to the podium to introduce them to the student body. Announcements followed next. After assembly, the prefects led us to our classrooms. And so began five years of my life in a Catholic education boarding high school.

Boarding life was strict. I had trouble settling into high school life and started acting up and breaking rules. I struggled with staying still in class for long periods, and I often got into trouble with teachers, who disliked my rebellious and playful attitude. My maths teacher, in particular, Mr Bob Wilson, hated my disruptive behaviour in class. I remember him instructing us one morning, "Don't touch any of the paper and scissors I gave you until I tell you to."

I had already started cutting up the paper in the shape of a girl. When he realised what I was up to, he stormed towards me and snatched the paper from my hands, almost knocking me to the ground. "What do you think you're doing? Didn't I tell you not to touch the paper?" he shouted in frustration.

I giggled and gave him a defiant stare.

"That's it. Get out!" he shouted. My punishment was to stand outside the class for the rest of the lesson. I strolled out of class, relieved, and stood by the window where he had instructed me to stand. I made silly faces and signalled my friend to join me. When the maths lesson finished, Mr Wilson gave me a stern talking to and threatened to report me to Father John if I continued my unruly behaviour.

I also acted out and ended up in trouble during individual study times. The school program included study periods every afternoon and evening. Many of us disliked study periods. We used the time as an opportunity to talk and play.

One night, Father Arthur was on study duty. He was a tough disciplinarian. He taught us English literature, including William Shakespeare. We had nicknamed him Banquo, after the ghost in Macbeth. He had the habit of appearing like a vision at the classroom window during study, watching classroom activity without us realising he was there. On occasion, we could sense his presence by the smell of his cigarettes.

That particular evening, I got chatting with my classmate Phillip instead of doing work. Phillip was lanky and very intelligent. He was a few years older than me and treated me like his younger sister. He often helped me with subjects I found difficult. On this evening, many of us in class played around, laughing and cracking jokes instead of studying.

Suddenly, the room went dead silent. I did not pay much attention. I had my back to the window, engrossed in mucking about. Then Phillip nudged me with his elbow.

"Ouch, what did you do that for?" I asked, laughing.

He tilted his head towards the window. I sensed trouble and whirled around.

Banquo was standing still at the large open window; his small watery eyes fixated on me, a burning cigarette clasped between his lips. *Shite, how long has he been there!*

He beckoned me with his middle finger. I scampered out of the class to where he was standing on the veranda. He had a large stick in his hand. I knew the drill and stuck out my hand for the lashing. What he did next took me by surprise.

He removed the cigarette from his mouth, held it between his fingers, stepped forward, and stood so close to me our noses almost touched. I could see the large, open pores on his ruddy skin, and I could smell the alcohol on his breath as he huffed. My instinct was to turn and run, but I didn't dare move. His bluish-grey eyes pierced into mine. *That's strange. He's not angry*! I remember thinking.

"What are you doing with that tall, stupid guy called Phillip?" he asked. The question came out of the blue.

I gulped and stepped back, fighting to compose myself. "N...no... nothing, Father," I stammered.

"He's not good for you. Stay away from him. You understand?" he said, as he peered through the window at Phillip.

I nodded, puzzled, as his gaze turned back towards me.

He jabbed me in the ribs with the stick. "Go back to your desk. I better not catch you with him again. Next time I won't let you off as easy," he said.

With that, he stuck his almost burnt-out cigarette back between his lips, swivelled around, and wandered away into the dark, puffing, smoke billowing behind his stocky body.

I stumbled back to my desk, hand on my mouth, still stunned. *Did that happen?* My classmates, who had been watching, were just as astounded.

A furious debate about what just happened ensued; some thought he was drunk and decided not to bother punishing me. Others reckoned he thought Phillip was my boyfriend and was warning me. Either way, I knew I had got off pretty easy. Banquo was not lenient. Under normal circumstances, he would have either lashed me or sent me to Father John's office for extra discipline. That incident spooked me.

As it was, Phillip was not my boyfriend. I had many platonic, fantastic friends who were boys. Some of them, like Philip, treated me like their younger sister.

They used to buy me lollies and soft drinks at the school tuck shop. I loved stork sweets, which are similar to today's lollipops, and soon they gave me the nickname Stork, which stuck into my adulthood.

I did not have a boyfriend until my last year in high school. That did not last long, anyway. We were more suited as good friends.

I had many close disciplinary calls throughout my five years at high school, and sometimes I did not think I would complete my studies. I hated the strict, stifling rules of the Catholic college. It's a wonder Father John did not suspend me.

The one time I came close to suspension was towards my final high school exams when I got drunk. Father John had given four of us permission to go into town for the afternoon. On our way back, Peter, my classmate, produced a bottle of cheap brandy and offered us a drink.

I had never drunk before, so I refused. They all egged me on, and I relented, not wanting to appear uncool. The brandy was bitter as we took turns passing the bottle around, taking large, quick gulps. Not long after, I started feeling dizzy.

The giggling started as we staggered back to college. We arrived at dinner time and proceeded to the dining hall, where we made absolute fools of ourselves. Kuki saw us and led me away to the dormitory.

The Matron reported us to Father John. He summoned us to his office the following morning and told us he had considered suspending us but had reconsidered because we were close to our final exams. Instead, he punished us by making us wash the dining hall tables for one month. I showed my gratitude to him by becoming a model student for the rest of my time at high school.

Despite my struggles with discipline, life in high school was not all dreary. I enjoyed subjects like English, history, biology and domestic science. I found the way those subjects were taught engaging, and I related better to the teachers. I learnt to cook, sew, knit, and crochet, all of which have come in handy later in life.

I was good at sports and played softball for the school team. I also became a member of the ballroom dancing club, which I loved.

I completed high school in November 1974 and travelled back home to await the results.

CONTEXT AND REFLECTION

Having grown up in a sometimes-difficult home environment, I often acted out in negative ways to get attention.

The school environment, with its complexities and harsh discipline, did not help. I had difficulty distinguishing right from wrong and became rebellious and anti-establishment.

I had internalised the anger and punishment I saw around me, and I sought to create that environment in my life. I seemed to thrive in chaotic environments.

Chapter 7

The Challenges of Adulthood

"Emotional agility means being aware and accepting of all your emotions, even learning from the most difficult ones. It means getting beyond conditioned or pre-programmed cognitive and emotional responses (your hooks), to live in the moment with a clear reading of present circumstances, respond appropriately and then act in alignment with your deepest values."

—Susan David.

I spent nine months at home in Francistown waiting for my high school results and admission to university. I was sixteen. While waiting, I applied for a temporary job at the old African School. It was now a community high school for troubled teenagers struggling with mainstream schooling. Fancy me getting a job there. How ironic!

I clutched my job-acceptance letter to my body as I skipped towards the staffroom on my first day. I waltzed into the staffroom to the teachers' curious stares; many of them were much older than I and no doubt wondered who this young upstart was.

"Good morning," I announced. "I'm the new Setswana teacher."

I felt all grown up. I enjoyed the teaching job. I got along well with the students, and I was thrilled that they looked up to me. Many of them were almost the same age as me, and I could relate to their issues. I was able to motivate them to take their studies seriously.

A few months into my teaching job, I started a romantic relationship. Casper and I met one afternoon as I walked home from work. That was the start of my first real romantic relationship. This dark-skinned, handsome and sexy boy who exuded confidence with his every move impressed me. His raspy voice struck a chord as he introduced himself. He was easy to talk to and very funny. I liked his boldness and streetwise manner.

Cas, as I called him, was two years older than me. He grew up in Francistown. His family had settled in Botswana from South Africa. His father was a Pentecostal church pastor, and they lived in Maipaahela, a location on the western side of the river. Though I had often seen him around town, I had never spoken to him. Rumours circulated that Cas had been expelled from high school for fighting.

We started meeting after school, and he walked me home. I would pack my books in a hurry when the last school bell rang and dash to the school gate, eager for his familiar captivating smile. I loved our strolls along the dirt road, holding hands with not a care in the world.

One day he invited me to come and watch him play football on Saturday. He was the goalkeeper for "Tafa," one of two top local soccer teams in Francistown.

My excitement was uncontainable as I invited Kuki and my friends to come along on Saturday afternoon. The noise and the rising dust hit us before we turned the corner towards the football ground. We sprinted forward in wild excitement as the dusty ground, packed to capacity with hordes of screaming, unruly soccer fanatics, came into view. The place was buzzing.

Tafa was playing against "Tafic," the other top team. Their rivalry was legendary. The loud sound of singing and stomping, coupled with the incessant beating of drums at each end of the ground, added to the charged and hypnotic atmosphere. A solid mass of men and women stood in front of us, pushing and shoving at each other, everyone jostling for the best viewpoint.

With our arms clasping each other tight, we plunged into the heaving mass, navigating our way through the throng of bodies. We stomped on others' feet, pushed and shoved, and made our way to where the Tafa supporters stood. We wanted to stand close to the goal post, to have a magnificent view of Cas.

The crowd was wild as the referees led the teams into the field, Tafa wearing black and white and Tafic in red and white. We joined the deafening chants of the Tafa fans, screaming and cheering at the top of our lungs, determined to outdo the other team.

My heart jumped out of my chest in pride as I watched Cas walk out with his team. His athletic build and excellent physique were on full display.

The match got underway. It was electric to watch Cas as he jumped and stretched and threw himself about to prevent Tafic from scoring. The game was a smash. Tafa won the game three-nil. I had no hope of seeing Cas after the match—the crowds were unstoppable and swamped the team, jostling to meet the players.

We made our way through the dispersing crowd. It was late afternoon, and we had to get back home. I was on cloud nine as we danced our way back home, still exhilarated.

Cas came over to see me later that evening. He had phoned to say he would wait for me outside the front gate of our house. He looked tired but exhilarated. We strolled around the streets, holding hands. We kissed and cuddled. His attractiveness had me in a spell, and I guess seeing him in his element today cemented my feelings for him.

Though Kuki liked Cas, she had her reservations about him. "Be careful with Casper," she said. "Just watch him, okay?"

"Okay, Kuki. Don't fuss, please." She irritated me. I was sure she envied me because her boyfriend was not as handsome as Cas.

Cas started coming over to our house to visit almost daily. Sometimes he took us to Mophane club, a popular music joint close to home.

He soon became a part of the scene of our many high school friends who lived in Francistown. We strolled a lot around town or visited friends' homes to chill and listen to music. Cas exuded confidence. My friends liked him but had reservations about him—no doubt because of his reputation. He frightened them, though he was always on his best behaviour in front of them.

To me, he was fantastic. We became inseparable. I had my first sexual experience with Cas at home one day when my parents had gone away to their cattle post.

Papa had bought land and established a cattle post at Makobeng, a rural cattle grazing area about five hours' drive from Francistown. The cattle post had a borehole, two large kraals, and some mud dwellings. Papa kept two hundred head of cattle and fifty goats at the cattle post. He hired two local men to look after the livestock. The cattle post was his pride and joy, and he and Mum went there often. On this occasion, they were away for two days.

That evening, we lounged about with some friends listening to rock music. At midnight they all started leaving. Kuki stayed for a little while. Out of sheer exhaustion, she crawled off to bed. Cas and I stayed back listening to *Electric Ladyland* by Jimi Hendrix. He moved from where he was sitting and squeezed himself on the one-seater where I was.

I turned to mush as his warm body connected with mine. As we started kissing, I knew this time was different. I was ready. We moved outside to the large tree outside the kitchen and lay on the blanket I had snuck from the bedroom when Kuki was in the toilet. Cas was gentle and kept whispering sweet little loving words in my ear to help me relax.

I shivered with fear and was nervous with anticipation. The sex was a nerve-wracking, confusing experience—

made worse because it was at home, and I didn't want to get caught! Cas was more experienced than I was and guided me through it all. He taught me all I needed to know about sex.

He was a great and considerate lover and always made sure we used protection. Something else I had no clue about. I learned a lot from him. I enjoyed having sex with Cas, but I worried about falling pregnant. A few of my girlfriends had become pregnant. I knew Papa would be unforgiving if that happened.

Mum discovered my affair with Cas soon after. I walked into the house from a walk with Cas. I knew by her stiff posture and pursed lips that she was cross about something. She had been waiting for me.

"Why are you going out with this worthless high school dropout?" she asked.

I hated it when she was judgemental of other people. We had many arguments about her habit of thumbing her nose at others.

"He's only a friend, Mum."

"Rubbish. I know he is your boyfriend. He is not someone to associate with. I want you to stop seeing him."

From that day, I started meeting with Cas away from home. Sometimes I used my friends as decoys, pretending I was visiting their house, when in fact, I was going out with Cas. Sometimes Cas snuck into our home when my parents were away. As the saying goes, forbidden love is sweet. My relationship with Cas was as strong as ever. I felt Mum resented that I was giving someone else more attention than I was to her. She was suffocating me in her demand for attention.

I continued my temporary job at the high school until my university acceptance letter came through. "Guess what, Cas, I have exciting news," I said.

"What? Tell me," he said, curious.

"My letter of university admission arrived yesterday."

"Oh, when do you go?" he asked, not sounding enthusiastic.

"In a few weeks."

"Congratulations. That's splendid news for you, but what does that mean for us?"

I was cautious with my response. "We can continue seeing each other. You can come to Gaborone to visit, and of course, I'll come home during holidays."

"I can get a job in Gaborone. We'll be able to see each other daily," he said.

I hesitated. "I don't think that would work, Cas. I don't think there are many jobs in Gaborone. Also, I'll be busy with studies and not have time to meet daily."

His frustrated look said it all. "I'm sure I can get something. Let's not talk about it now," he said.

I tried to conceal my excitement so as not to hurt him. I could tell the news was hitting him hard. As a high school dropout, he did not have many prospects of getting a job except for a few unskilled casual jobs that he sometimes got around town. He still lived at home and depended on his parents for his living expenses. I steered clear of asking him to go back to school because he was touchy whenever I raised this subject.

As my time to leave drew closer, tension built between us as we tried to work out the way forward. We argued a lot. He exploded at minor things. I knew he was thinking of the implications. My going away to university was the death knell for our relationship, much to Mum's relief. She suspected we still saw each other in secret.

Cas accompanied me on the train journey to Gaborone. The train was full with many students from surrounding high schools making the journey to university.

I explored around the train and met Gemma, who was also on her way to start her first year. Her endearing smile and beautiful, open face captured me. She was full-bodied, gorgeous, and self-assured.

"Hi there, I'm Anna, but my friends call me Stork," I said.

"Hi, Stork. I'm Gemma. Are you going to University?"

"Yeah, what about you?"

"Oh, yes. I'm so excited. The admission took forever to come through. Which high school are you from?"

"St Joseph's. What about you?"

"Gaborone Secondary School. I used to go to St Joseph's to play netball."

"Did you? I don't recall seeing you. Are you from Francistown as well?"

"Yes, my family live in White City. It's so great to meet someone from Francistown, going to the University as well. I was hoping for that."

"Come on to my compartment. My boyfriend Cas is there. You can meet him," I encouraged.

She followed me to the compartment. Gemma and I clicked and soon discovered a shared passion for clothes and fashion. We were both into tight bell-bottomed pants, tank tops, and stilettos. I related Mum's futile attempts at getting me to dress in conservative below-the-knee skirts and dresses. She howled in laughter, tears streaming down her beautiful face when I described Mum's attempt to convince me to wear a girdle.

Gemma had a quirky sense of self-deprecating humour, mixed with gentleness. I found this a very endearing quality. I was elated to have met her. I was about to start university life with a solid, dependable friend.

Cas stayed with friends when we got to Gaborone. I lived on campus, busy settling in and starting lectures. He wanted us to meet daily and did not understand when I told him I couldn't see him because of lectures. He got mad.

I started resenting having to divide my time between trying to fit into campus life and seeing Cas daily. Our relationship became rockier. He became jealous and controlling and was loud and argumentative whenever he came to visit on weekends. We had many fights. After one public and embarrassing spat, he came pretty close to hitting me and threatened me with a knife. He was that kind of person.

He travelled back to Francistown. I missed him, but I was relieved he had left. I felt conflicted about our relationship. We broke up when I was back home for holidays.

Gemma and I had secured rooms in Block A, a medium-sized brick residential building for first-year students. The block comprised a row of eight twin-share rooms facing each other, separated by a small courtyard with a well-kept lawn. A covered, narrow veranda ran along each side of the courtyard, with benches outside the rooms. At the end of the block stood a large shared bathroom with multiple toilets, showers, and washbasins. Unlike my high school, the university had cleaning staff who ensured that all campus areas were spotless.

My roommate was Sandy, a dark-skinned, slender, and beautiful girl. Gemma's room, which she shared with Bonnie, was across the courtyard, opposite ours. We were all making friends. I met Leila, whom I recognised from our primary school days in Francistown. She had left midway through primary school when her father moved overseas for work. We had lost touch. She was back in Botswana to start university.

Leila looked stunning in tight Levi jeans and a shirt that revealed perfect cleavage and perfect skin. She was very sexy and spoke English with a foreign accent, which she sometimes switched to Setswana. She was pretty and sophisticated, and she intimidated most of us. *Girl, you need to step up your game if you're to keep up!* I made a mental note to myself.

Gemma and I befriended Brie and Joyce. Brie was tall and slender with a fluid gazelle-like gait. Joyce was the exact opposite. She was of medium build, bubbly and loud. She could tell a cracker of a joke.

We spent a lot of time together as we attended similar lectures. We often walked to the dining hall together at mealtimes, and sometimes in the evenings, we studied in the library. Having fantastic friends made campus life interesting and enjoyable and not so daunting.

The university community had students from high schools around Botswana as well as South Africa, Swaziland, Lesotho, Ghana, and Zimbabwe. The diversity of cultures created a very interesting, dynamic mix of students. Life felt exciting and free. At the start of each semester, the Government gave us a generous stipend and book subsidy while supplying us with free tuition, accommodation, and meals. Many students, I included, blew their stipend on alcohol and clothes.

CONTEXT AND REFLECTION

I had no internal emotional resilience to interpret and deal with adult life's challenges and its ever-changing environment. I had no clue about which direction I wanted my life to go.

Going to university was an opportunity for me to grow and discover myself, a journey that did not come easily for me. I was immature and ill-equipped to deal with the challenges of young adulthood. I depended on others to point the way forward for me. My life was shallow and revolved around lectures and partying.

Chapter 8

When Hope Is Lost

"Love only hurts when you have a belief that has provided you with a limited perspective of yourself and your reality."

—*Mike Dooley*

Life was different when I returned for the third year in September 1977. Jake was long gone. His acrimonious ending of our relationship left me broken and alone. My world had taken a three-hundred-sixty degree turn for the worse.

"My God, Stork, you look so thin. Are you ok?" asked Leila.

"No, Lei, I'm still sad because of what happened. Papa was furious. He came close to disowning me."

"That's bad. Look, it's over now. You need to move on," she laughed, looking me over.

I smiled at her. "I'll be ok. I need time."

"Try to put it behind you."

Much as my friends tried to cheer me up, I could not pick myself up. I put up a brave face and bottled my genuine feelings, trying as much as possible to satisfy everyone, even though my spirit shattered into a million little pieces.

Inside I was a fragile, hurting mess. Party nights became my solace as I started drinking and smoking to cope. I had casual relationships, but nothing worked. I just did not care anymore.

One Friday night, we got invited to a party in Tom's room. Tom was one of a group of older students we called "The Mature." They were working men with families and had taken leave to pursue further studies. Students liked them, as they provided expensive drinks—scotch, brandy, gin, you name it—at their parties. The celebration was in full swing when we arrived; the tiny room was packed. People packed into every conceivable space. Gemma, Joyce, Leila, and I squeezed into the room. Tom offered us gin and tonic, and before long, I lost count of how many drinks I had. Every time I looked, someone topped up my glass. I lost track of time and did not remember us leaving the party.

"Stork, your room is there." I saw a dim outline of someone. I blinked hard to focus. Wayne, Sandy's boyfriend, sat on a bench opposite my room, watching as I tried to unlock a door to what I believed was my room. He was a fourth-year student and socialised with us at parties. He was brotherly and caring, often looking out for us. He did not drink. He came over and grabbed my key. He took my hand and led me to my room. He opened the door, ushered me in, and put the key in the inside lock. I heard his footsteps fade away after I locked the door.

I tried to undress, failed, and passed out on the bed. I woke up mid-morning the following day and dragged myself to the bathroom for a shower. After dressing, I went and knocked on Gemma's door. From her unkempt state, I could see she had just crawled out of bed.

"Stork, what happened last night?" she asked, holding her head and groaning in pain, her eyes bloodshot.

I tried to laugh, but I could not. The persistent, pounding pain in my head was too much. "I don't remember. That's why I'm here."

Bonnie, Gemma's roommate, was sitting on her bed. She looked at us and laughed. "You two are pathetic. You all came staggering and singing at the top of your voices. Stork and Joyce left to find their rooms while you, Gemma, and Leila dashed to the bathroom to spew. It was quite a scene. I helped you and Lei off the bathroom floor!" she said, nodding her head at Gemma.

"I remember Wayne opening my room," I said.

"Yes, he was leaving Sandy's room when you lot came," Bonnie said.

The hangover was unbearable. My mouth was dry, and my body dehydrated. Gemma and I dragged ourselves to the tuck shop to get soft drinks. The partying was getting out of control.

End of year academic exams were fast approaching; it was May 1978. I had missed lectures and not studied much.

I turned up for a psychology exam one morning, and the lecturer approached me, "Hello, young lady. You're in the wrong room," he said.

I popped outside, checked the room number again, and walked back in. "I'm in the correct room. I'm supposed to take the exam for this subject," I said.

Puzzled, he scanned his list and found my name. He looked at me in astonishment. "I have never seen you in my lectures before."

I nodded yes, sheepish. I had only ever attended a handful of lectures at the beginning of the semester, and then I stopped.

He admitted me into the exam room and kept staring at me, shaking his head. It was embarrassing. I sat and blundered my way through most of the questions. Of course, I could not finish the paper. The end-of-year results came out when I was home in Francistown. I had failed the third year. Some of my party friends had also failed, and the university had discontinued them. *That's it*, I remember thinking, *I'm next*. Gemma, Brie, and Joyce had completed their Diploma and left to start their teaching careers.

The disastrous third-year result was a defining moment for me. The university phoned to let me know they were giving me a chance to repeat the third year. Somehow, they believed I had the potential. Their gesture stunned and humbled me. That was the break I needed. Something inside me told me to stand up and prove my worth to myself. I always knew I had the capability, but no motivation.

When I went back for my second bite at third year, I stopped drinking and concentrated on my studies. My lecturers, well aware of my partying ways, were doubtful that I would succeed. I imagined them taking bets to see if I would last the distance. I set out to prove them wrong.

I hung out with new friends, serious students who were not into partying. They did not judge me. Instead, they became great, supportive mates. I worked my guts out that year.

"Mum, my third-year results are out," I said one day when Mum came home for lunch. I was again at home, having completed my third year. She held her breath and looked at me, anxious. "I have passed. I'm proceeding to my last year."

Mum jumped in excitement and gave me a spontaneous hug and a smooch. This open show of ecstatic emotion was a very rare thing with her. I was proud of myself, but I knew the tough battle was ahead. I had faith. Papa was cautiously happy, but not as openly demonstrative of his pride. Our relationship was still difficult.

My fourth and final year was bone-breaking hard work. One of my lecturers, Dr Muliwa, took me under his wing and mentored me. He pushed me hard. He summoned me one evening and set me straight.

"Listen, Anna, the university gave you a last chance. I've committed to supervising you because I believe in your potential. Don't disappoint me" It was a sobering moment.

In 1980, I completed my last year's exams and received a post to teach at Swaneng Hill School, a high school in Serowe village. I was 23. My results were not yet out. Swaneng Hill School, as the name says, was on top of a hill, about five kilometres from the centre of Serowe.

I loved my job. I taught English and History. Many of the students came from disadvantaged families and walked for miles to attend class, often in foul weather. The responsibility of guiding and shaping their young minds was immense. I loved seeing these youngsters, who had very little in their lives, committed to getting an education to better themselves.

Thirty teachers taught at the school, and I recognised some of them from university days. Some teachers were expatriates. We formed a great, supportive school community. Serowe did not offer much entertainment, except for a local disco hall and a small bar near the school. We often met at the bar for drinks or threw house parties.

On my way home from class one afternoon, I recognised Dr Muliwa's white station wagon snaking its way along the rough gravel road towards the teacher's quarters.

He stopped beside me and got out. "I thought I better come and relay the news myself," he said, giving me a warm hug. "Your results are out. You have passed your degree with merit. I knew you had it in you!"

I did not know whether to rejoice or cry. I had done it! What a great morale booster! I was honoured that he had driven all the way to come and congratulate me. I think he was also in shock!

Dr Muliwa stayed in Serowe overnight. A few of us took him to the local bar for a drink. We spent the evening sharing grand stories of life and adventures at the university. I did not see him the following morning when he left. I often think of his dedication and kindness to me. He helped me navigate a very tricky period of my life.

A year after I started teaching, I began taking driving lessons. My driving instructor was an elderly Motswana man. He taught me to drive in a beaten-up old Datsun 123. The car brakes were erratic, and I had many hair-raising moments trying to brake in traffic. I persevered, and I got my driver's license—a rite of passage for me.

Six months after getting my license, I got a government loan to buy my first car, a brand new, emerald green Toyota Corolla-Sprinter. I was very proud of myself as I drove to Francistown for the school holidays, and I couldn't wait to show the car to my parents. Mum danced with joy. To her, this was a sign that I was growing up and becoming mature.

Papa had retired from education and was running a transportation business in Bobonong and his cattle post in Makobeng. He got to see the car when he came home one weekend. He was very proud of me.

I now found life at home quiet and dreary whenever I went to visit. My siblings were away for either work or study. Few people came to visit our house. My parents had few friends and seldom visited anyone, not even the neighbours.

My relationship with Mum was difficult. She was dependent and demanding of my attention, which I found exhausting. I loved her very much, but I felt I always had to please her to get her to love me.

CONTEXT AND REFLECTION

The circumstances that led to the breakup of my relationship with Jake had left me no direction, and instead, I masked my pain, which did not help my situation.

To find myself, I realised the only way forward was to persevere and work hard. Somehow, through perseverance and determination, I found the strength in me to pull myself together and concentrate on my studies.

I had a professional job and was doing well career-wise, but I was still empty inside.

Chapter 9

A New Era

"If you want to move to another room, you have to get up and move step by step in that direction. Just sitting in your chair and demanding that you be in the other room will not work. It's the same thing. We all want our problem to be over with, but we do not want to do the small things that will add up to the solution."

—Louise Hay

The Chief Education Officer in the Ministry of Education telephoned me around midday on a warm sunny day in 1985. It was school vacation, and I was in Francistown visiting my parents.

"Hello, is that Anna?" came the voice across the phone.

"Yes, it is."

"This is Mrs Mogaladi, from the Department of Education. I'm ringing to let you know we have offered you a two-year scholarship to study for a master's degree in Sydney, Australia."

"Thank you, Mrs Mogaladi. But why Australia? I thought I was going to the United Kingdom."

"I know we had floated that idea; however, this scholarship came through first. We thought you would be the best person for it."

"Thank you very much. Which university am I going to? When do I leave?"

"You are going to Sydney University, and you leave in six weeks." I knew little about Australia.

I told my parents the news at lunchtime. "Mum, Papa, I have some news," I said, still in shock but delighted. "The Government has offered me a two-year scholarship to study in Australia."

"Oh my God," Mum said, placing her hand across her mouth, enormously shocked.

Though I had always dreamt of studying overseas, I was also in shock. The departure date was too soon.

"Congratulations, Anna. That's an outstanding achievement, my child," Papa said, beaming.

He was now back in Francistown. He had heart complications and high blood pressure and had had to stop his transportation business due to ill health. Mum had taken over responsibility for the cattle post.

Papa was very disappointed about having to give up running the transportation business and the cattle post. He now spent most of his time between doctor's visits and resting at home. He found that lifestyle challenging as he had always been an active person.

I drove back to Swaneng to gather my belongings and say goodbye. My friends organised a large truck to transport my furniture to Francistown and hosted a big farewell send-off. It was stressful to leave my friends and my students. However, going overseas was the fresh start I craved. It was the opportunity to leave the negative past behind me.

I stayed home for the next few weeks before I left. I kept myself busy rearranging the furniture in my parents' house to squeeze in my personal household goods from Swaneng. I further used the time to dispose of old stuff.

Though it pleased my parents I was going for further studies, my imminent departure made them sad and concerned. Few people in Botswana travelled to Australia in those days.

While I was waiting to leave for Australia, I spent time with Papa, and we had in-depth conversations. Papa and I had a love-hate relationship. Shared similar characteristics, such as our love of history, literature, and music, bonded us. We share the same star sign, Aquarius.

In primary school, I joined the school choir, and he used to come and watch me sing at school concerts. When we got home, he would call Kuki and me and join us to sing his favourite songs from the choir.

It was through him I developed a love for history and literature. I learned a lot about the history of Botswana and our family roots from him. He was a superb storyteller, always making unfamiliar concepts easy to understand—I suppose because he was a trained schoolteacher. I remember sitting on his lap when I was around eight and listening to him reading the story of Julius Caesar to me. I developed a love for the story. In no time, I could recite sections of Julius Caesar in full. He had a way of making words come alive that ignited a love for storytelling and teaching inside me. That could be one reason I excelled at English literature and ended up studying linguistics. He was my hero, and I always wanted him to be proud of me.

Our relationship confused me. I disliked his authoritarian side and the way he treated Mum when we were young. I sometimes found it hard to reconcile his different sides and to see beyond his shortcomings. Though I admired him, I held deep-seated anger towards him.

My relationship with Papa was further complicated by Mum, who took every opportunity to paint a horrible picture of him. I think our closeness upset her, and she fought to sever the powerful bond that I had with him. The pressure to take sides between them distressed me. I loved them both and did not want to choose between them.

The weeks leading to my departure allowed us to mend our broken relationship. We spent hours sitting under the shade of the large tree in the backyard, chatting.

"We'll miss you when you go, Anna. How do you feel about going to Australia?" he asked one morning.

"I'm nervous, Papa. I know nothing about the place."

"Don't worry, my daughter. I'm sure it will go well. I know little about Australia also, except that it's very far. At least the people there speak English."

"Yes, that's an enormous advantage. I don't know how I'll cope with the long flight, though, seeing that I've never flown in a jumbo jet."

"You'll get used to it. I remember feeling the same when I flew to Kampala, Uganda. I ended up enjoying the flight."

"Yes, I remember that time. Were you lonely in Kampala?"

"Sometimes. I missed home very much, but I made friends which helped."

"Thanks, Papa. I must admit it's exciting to be going for my master's."

"Yes, it's a great opportunity. Two years is a long time, though. I just hope I'll still be alive when you return, my child," he sighed.

"Please don't say that Papa, I'm sure you'll be ok. You are under good medical care now."

I now realised his vulnerability. He was a shadow of his former imposing personality. These in-depth father to daughter chats were precious to me. It was rare to see this tender loving side of Papa, and I cherished it. He was a typical old-school African father, uncomfortable showing emotion and vulnerability to his children. I realised it took much for him to open up. We never talked like that again. When I returned from Australia three years later, he was very ill and frail.

Before I left, Mum insisted we visit one of the faith healers to get a blessing for my journey. I agreed. We drove sixty kilometres out of Francistown to the tiny village of Mmandunyane, where Rre Peter, a spiritual healer, lived. On our journey, we passed through dense forest on a narrow, sandy dirt track. Mum now drove a Toyota Hilux truck, which could handle the rough terrain.

People who lived in the region practised subsistence farming, kept livestock, and cultivated market crops. The rough road, mainly used by donkey driven scotch carts, was nearly impassable in parts. We came across several scotch carts on our way to Rre Peter's. They had to get off the road to allow Mum's Hilux to pass.

Rre Peter was sitting on a wooden stool outside one of three mud huts in his small compound. He was a light-skinned elderly man with a mop of white hair and a grey beard. He had discoloured and chapped hands from working on the small farming plot they kept near their dwelling. Rre Peter lived a meagre, self-subsistent rural life.

Unlike Mma Omponye, he did not have a grand church. He was low key but a master of his craft. What he lacked in material possessions, he made up for with exuberance. He was open, very chatty, and expressive. He stood up to welcome us as we arrived and invited us to sit on a low wooden stool next to him. His wife sat on a mat beside him.

"Welcome, Mma Manyaula," he said, mispronouncing Mum's name. From his animated face, you could tell he enjoyed having visitors.

"*Dumela* Rre Peter," Mum said.

"You came at the right time. Please join us for mealie meal and delele," Rre Peter said. Delele is a slimy vegetable abundant in the wild in particular areas of Botswana; it was one of my least favourite things to eat.

"Thanks, Rre Peter. I ate before we left. Anna, please have some," Mum said.

I stared at her, astonished. Mum had instructed us to never, ever eat food offered at faith healers' homes for hygiene reasons. Now she was putting me on the spot because it embarrassed her to refuse. She was also well aware that I hated delele.

"No, thank you. I ate before we left, too," I said.

She looked daggers at me. I stared her down.

"Are you sure you don't want to eat Mma?" Rre Peter's wife said to Mum.

"No thanks, Mma. We will have something to eat next time we come," Mum said, avoiding eye contact with Rre Peter's wife. They had really put her on the spot. I loved it!

Rre Peter got the message and got on to business. "How can we help today?" he asked.

"This young lady is going overseas. We have come to ask for blessings for a safe journey and that God protects her when she is there," Mum said.

Rre Peter turned towards me, brimming with curiosity. "Congratulations, young lady. You are travelling to faraway lands. Where are you going, England?"

"No, Rra, I'm going to Australia."

He looked perplexed.

I realised he didn't have a clue where Australia was. "I have never heard of the place. All we know about those faraway places is England. When do you leave?" he asked.

"Next week."

"We shall pray for you and protect you, my child. Your Mum has done the right thing by bringing you here." He turned to his wife, who sat listening, fascinated. "Mma, please prepare a bath." She stood up and disappeared into one hut.

When she came out, Rre Peter went into the hut. We could hear him chanting prayers. When he finished, he called me in. "Make sure you bathe from head to toe," he said.

A large tin bath surrounded by lit candles stood ready in the middle of the room. It was half-filled with greyish looking water. I stripped and dipped my toes in. The water was freezing. I got in and washed in a hurry. There was no towel, so I shook myself dry, trying to expel the excess water, dressed, and stepped outside to dry in the warm sun.

Rre Peter performed more blessing rituals and assured me I would be ok.

Mum paid him, then we said our goodbyes and drove back home. Mum was chatty during the drive back.

The following week Mum and Kuki drove me to Gaborone to see me off at the airport. Saying goodbye to them was very hard. We hugged as the departure announcement came through. It was a strange time for me. I had never been overseas, and I was nervous.

On the 26th of June 1986, I left Botswana on an afternoon Air Zimbabwe flight to Harare, the capital city of Zimbabwe. My connecting flight to Sydney was the following evening, so I stayed overnight at my brother Cecil's place. At that time, he was working for the Botswana High Commission in Harare.

He picked me up from the airport. "So, you're flying with Qantas tomorrow?"

"I guess so. Is that what they call the airline?"

"You mean you've never heard of Qantas, the national airline of Australia?"

"No, I know little about Australia."

He was stunned. Seeing how nervous I looked, he reassured me I would be ok. As a diplomat, he had travelled to many places worldwide and was comfortable with international travel. On the other hand, I found the prospect of leaving Botswana to travel overseas overwhelming.

The flight was long and stressful. This was my first experience in a jumbo jet, and I found it hard to sleep during the flight. I had an entire row of economy seats to myself, and I tried to stretch as best as I could. There was no other dark-skinned person on the flight, except for one African man I had glimpsed boarding in Harare. Everything on the plane was strange, from the flight attendants' accents to the food.

We arrived in Sydney on Saturday evening. A gentleman from AIDAB, the Australian Government body sponsoring my scholarship, met me, and drove me to my hotel. I asked him if there were Batswana students at Sydney University. He answered no. My heart sank. I was quiet for the rest of the drive.

The hotel was in Edgecliff, in the Eastern part of Sydney, near the train station. The long trip had exhausted me. All I wanted was to jump into bed and sleep. But I was starving. After checking me in, the AIDAB officer informed me he would pick me up on Monday morning at eight to take me to their office.

I had to get some food!

"I see there's a restaurant in the hotel. What time does it close?" I asked the receptionist.

"The restaurant does not open on the weekend, madam. There's a takeaway café across the street, next to the traffic signals. You can get some food there," he said.

I thanked him and took the elevator to my room to freshen up. I was nervous about going out to the takeaway cafe. I walked to the café and bought chicken and chips. The chicken tasted awful. I ended up eating the chips and throwing most of the chicken out. The food tasted different from the food back home. Even this small realisation made me feel alienated.

The following morning, I needed to go out and buy toiletries. I asked the room cleaner if there was a pharmacy nearby.

"Most places around here close on Sunday. Why don't you catch a train to Bondi Junction? More places are open there, including pharmacies," she said, in a hard to comprehend accent.

I thanked her, too scared and embarrassed to ask for further help—more complication. I did not know how to catch a suburban train! So, I did not go. I just had to make do with whatever meagre toiletries were provided by the hotel.

I was jet lagged and spent the entire day in my room sleeping. By night-time, I was wide awake. I stood by the window of my fifth-floor room for most of the night, watching whatever was going on in the street below.

The AIDAB officer came to pick me up on Monday morning, as he had promised. When I arrived at the office, another student was waiting there. "Anna, please meet Wimala. She's enrolled in the same masters of linguistics program as you," the officer said.

Wimala was from Sri Lanka and was a lot older than me. She looked very pleased to see me. "Hello, Wimala," I said as I shook her hand. "I'm glad I'm not the only new student."

"Me too. I'm so nervous. This is my first time overseas," she said.

It was a relief to realise I was not the only one petrified of leaving home and coming to a foreign land. We promised to help each other settle. As part of orientation, a staff member escorted us into the city to open bank accounts and show us how to use an Automatic Teller Machine. Everything was so new and foreign.

Wimala had arrived the week before me and had already found accommodation in the inner-city suburb of Newtown, closer to the main Sydney University campus. We parted ways as she hurried to catch a bus back to her accommodation.

An AIDAB staff member gave me directions to walk to nearby Central station to catch the train back to Edgecliff. She explained what I had to do to buy a ticket. It was a daunting experience. I walked to Central station, clutching the piece of paper with the instructions written on it. It was now around five in the evening, and trains were busy with the peak hour rush.

Someone showed me where to buy a ticket and which platform to go to. Another person on the train alerted me when we approached Edgecliff. The first day in Sydney ended. I had achieved something by myself and was pleased.

I made my way back on the train to the AIDAB offices the following morning. This time they gave me instructions to get on a bus to the suburb of Broadway, to meet my homestay host, Ross. He was waiting for me at the bus stop. "Hello, young Lady. My name is Ross. What's your name?"

"I'm Anna," I said. "Welcome to Sydney, Anna. I'll show you the accommodation. It's only a short walk from here." Ross was a lovely and kind older gentleman. We walked to his spacious flat, which had expensive furniture, and was within walking distance to the University. I rented a room in his flat, and he drove me to Edgecliff to get my stuff. Ross showed me where the shopping centre and the university were.

A few days later, I started lectures. I met more overseas students and became friends with Tembo from Tanzania. I was becoming more comfortable, though I missed home and my family. I rang home the day after I settled in my new accommodation. I burst into tears when Papa picked up the phone. He called Mum, who calmed me down. Six months after moving in with Ross, I found a bedsit in Newtown, again within walking distance to the university.

In the beginning, I found life in Sydney unwelcoming. I felt self-conscious and found the Australian accent hard to comprehend. Through Tembo, I met other African students studying at the University of New South Wales in Sydney. They used to host student gatherings and parties on the weekend.

It was at one of these parties I met Doug. He was not a student. He had been in Australia far longer than me and was working. Doug was interesting and carefree, and we hit it off. He was energetic, handsome, and loved to live life to the full. I found this quality appealing. We soon started an affair. He spent a lot of time in my tiny bedsit, and ultimately, I moved in with him. We had loads of fun together. He was easy going and funny.

A few months into our relationship, I found out I had an ectopic pregnancy. I ended up losing my left fallopian tube — a devastating and traumatic experience; the possibility of not conceiving worried me. A year after my ectopic pregnancy, we tried IVF. It was during this time that I applied for permanent residency.

After a few tries, I became pregnant with triplets but lost them at thirteen weeks. It was becoming clear I had problems carrying a pregnancy to term. However, I was too distressed to pursue a medical investigation into this. I was still studying and had to fully concentrate on completing my degree.

The stress of losing the pregnancy took a toll on our relationship. Things started turning sour between us. We often fought over small things, and I found this difficult. The relationship became unpleasant. Doug and I got along great, but we had significant differences that caused tension between us.

I thought leaving Botswana and making a fresh start in another environment would give me the emotional reprieve I craved. I was wrong. I ended up in another dysfunctional relationship.

I completed university in 1988, and I took a temporary job in a college in the city, teaching English to overseas students.

Nine months after I applied for permanent residency, the approval came. The approval was great, but I was now miserable in my relationship. I travelled back home to fulfil the government contract tied to my scholarship. Although I had permanent residency, I no longer intended to return to Australia.

CONTEXT AND REFLECTION

I had thought a change of environment would resolve my emotional issues.

In spite of moving to Australia, my life was not going the way I had hoped. I needed to change direction.

My thought pattern was still the same as it was in Botswana. Mentally, I was still sitting in the same old chair and not moving and yet expecting to be elsewhere.

At the time, I was not aware that unless I changed my perspective of life, I'd continue repeating the same patterns. I had to uncover and work on the root cause of why I attracted dysfunctional relationships.

I still struggled with defining myself, my values, and my direction in life.

Chapter 10

Back on the Roller Coaster

"The personality formed in the environment of coercive control is not well adapted to adult life. The survivor is left with fundamental problems in basic trust, autonomy, and initiative. She approaches the task of early adulthood—establishing independence and intimacy—burdened by major impairments in self-care, in cognition and in memory, in identity, and in the capacity to form stable relationships. She is still a prisoner of her childhood; attempting to create a new life, she reencounters the trauma."

—Judith Herman Lewis.

Arriving back in Botswana was a rude shock. Many things had changed.

Mum had accompanied Kuki to Gaborone to meet me at the airport. She could not hide her joy when she saw me. I cried when I saw them.

From the airport, we drove to Kuki's place in Palapye and stayed overnight. We caught up on news about the family, and it worried me to hear that Papa's health was declining.

The following morning, we drove to Francistown. When we arrived, Papa was sitting outside in his usual chair. When the car stopped, he stood up and shuffled towards us. He was very frail and looked ill.

I jumped out and ran to him. "Hello Papa," I said, giving him a warm hug.

He burst into tears as we embraced. "Welcome back, my child. I've been awake all night waiting for this moment."

I cried as I realised how sick and frail he was. I looked at Mum, wanting to comment on Papa's frailty. She was standing riveted at the car door, disdain written all over her face. That puzzled me, but I ignored it. Papa sat back in his chair, looking exhausted. We unloaded the luggage from the car and went outside and sat with Papa. Mum didn't join us. She closed herself in her room. She only came out at dinner time.

"Mum, you disappeared when we arrived. I thought you were going to join us outside," I said.

"Everything is fine. We had a long drive, so I wanted to rest," she said. She seemed aloof.

"Are you ok, Mum? You seem upset."

"I'm fine," she grumbled, not looking at me.

I left it; she was happier on the journey from the airport. Something must have upset her when we arrived. I retired early to sleep off the jet lag.

The following morning, I ran into Mum in the corridor and greeted her. She mumbled a response, not making eye contact. She was giving me the cold shoulder, and I could not work out why? It then dawned on me. She seemed infuriated by the warmth with which I greeted Papa. This cold treatment continued for a few days, and I started feeling rejected.

Kuki left to go back to Palapye, leaving me alone with my parents. The day after Kuki left, in sheer frustration, I talked to Papa. "Papa, what's going on? Ever since I arrived, Mum has been hostile."

"I don't know what's wrong with her, Anna. She has been ignoring me for a few days now."

"Well, I'm finding this frustrating and upsetting. Have I done something wrong? Why doesn't she speak to me?"

"You've done nothing wrong, my child. She's been acting strange. Maybe she doesn't like your affection towards me."

"Should I speak to her about it? I can't live with this tension."

"No, say nothing to her. Try to disregard her. Her nasty mood will blow over soon," Papa sighed.

It did not. Mum started putting me down over minor things.

"That's a tight skirt you are wearing today," she said one morning as I was getting ready to go into town.

"Oh, come on, Mum, it's not that tight." I laughed it off.

She walked away, irritated. Later, she made another snide remark about the meal I had prepared.

This time I wasn't having it. "Mum, have you got a problem with me? Ever since I came, you've been cold and not talking to me. What have I done wrong?" I angrily asked.

"Who said you have done anything wrong? Not every-thing is about you, Anna. I'm just quiet. That's all."

"But you have been making unpleasant remarks about my dress style and my cooking."

"You're just being sensitive."

As Papa had advised, I tried to avoid her, but it was difficult. We clashed over almost everything. The stress of the situation was taking its toll on me.

Not only was I dealing with readjustment issues, but I also had to deal with Mum's moods. She treated me like a stranger. I tried my best to please her, to no avail. Papa tried his best to chat with me, but I could tell he was nervous about being seen to be too close to me.

The tables of control between Mum and Papa had turned. He now depended on her as his primary carer. The considerable power he used to yield had disappeared.

"Don't you dare talk to me like that," she said to him many times. "I'm the one who's looking after you in your old age."

Papa often got very frustrated but kept quiet.

I had few friends to call on for support. Most of them had moved on with their lives. The only one I often saw was

Gemma. I saw little of my siblings, except for Kuki, whom I regularly visited, just to get away.

I was at home for four months while the Ministry of Education was sorting out my deployment. They had frozen my salary because of an overpayment error while I was away studying. I had no income and was living on my savings. Per the standard protocol, the ministry maintained my salary while I studied, and the overpayment came because I had stayed in Australia at the end of my studies, waiting for my permanent residency.

My clearance letter eventually arrived. I was assigned to Molepolole College of Education; the college trained high school teachers. It was a great relief to leave the tension at home and drive to the village of Molepolole, where the college was located. I packed up my Toyota Corolla, which I had left at home during my time in Australia, and made the six-hour drive to Molepolole.

Fitting in at the training college was hard. The principal assigned me to the languages department as a syntax and semantics lecturer. I also had to develop an English language curriculum for the second teacher training college, which was to open the following year in Tonota, a village close to Francistown.

The academic staff at Molepolole College included Batswana, British, American, Zambian, Zimbabwean, and Ghanaian lecturers. Most of the Batswana lecturers were my former University of Botswana colleagues. When I first arrived, I got along with almost all of them.

However, I soon discovered there were camps among staff, expatriates against local lecturers. Staff ideologies of how the college was operating clashed. One afternoon an argument broke out in a staff meeting about the standard of teaching at the college.

After a few terse exchanges between staff, I interjected. "Can I ask what the college is using as a measure of its course standard?"

The vice-principal, a Motswana lady, stared at me. "What do you mean? A standard is a standard."

"But we measure a standard against something. For instance, are you using the University of Botswana degrees to set the bar for the college diplomas?" I asked, much to her chagrin.

Some expatriate teachers nodded, agreeing with me, many with cynical smiles. One commented, "This is what we have been saying for ages. It's refreshing to get a new staff member who gets the point."

I was not aware that this topic had caused much division and hostility among staff before. The rest of the staff meeting was tense, and the issue was not resolved.

Following the staff meeting, I tried hard to remain non-aligned, but my innocent question had displeased local staff, who thought I was in collusion with the expatriates.

Some of them ostracised me—it was strange to experience alienation by my own people. I had left Australia feeling alienated and alone, and yearning for acceptance by my people and culture. In irony, I was now experiencing alienation and judgment by those I thought would embrace me.

My first anxiety attack took me by surprise. I was driving to a seminar in Selibe-Phikwe, a mining town in Botswana's central district, where I was to give a talk. I remember a powerful urge to get out of the car and just bolt; I fought hard to control the urge. I had never heard of anxiety, so I had no reference point. My initial thought was that I was losing my mind. I drove for two terrifying hours, and when I arrived in town, I drove straight to the local clinic.

The nurse in charge was Kuki's friend. I described my symptoms. "What you've experienced is an anxiety attack," she said.

I burst into tears. "I feel like I'm going mad," I said to her.

"You're not mad. Anxiety is common and can happen when we're under tremendous stress." Her explanation made sense. She prescribed me Valium.

When I got back to the college, the attacks returned and intensified. In hindsight, the stress of settling in a hostile environment where Mum rejected me and being rejected by fellow lecturers was getting to me.

I took time off work and travelled home to seek help from my parents. I stayed with Kuki for a few days. She helped me understand my anxiety. We drove to Francistown together.

The talk with my parents was unhelpful. Kuki and I came into the living room where Mum and Papa were sitting.

"Anna has been having anxiety attacks," Kuki said, facing both of them. They were silent for a little while.

Then Mum asked me. "Why have you got anxiety?"

"I don't know, Mum. I have had a lot of stress since I arrived, and I'm finding it difficult to readjust to life back in Botswana." I said, almost in tears. It was like I had done something wrong.

"Just readjust," she said. Again, I sensed she thought I was causing trouble.

"It's not that easy," Kuki said. "She has been through a rough time."

The conversation did not end well. Mum still insisted I settle down and get my act together. I became angry. I felt unheard, and I had had enough of the ill-treatment.

I got back to Molepolole very frustrated. The following six months were stressful. I struggled with anxiety and trying to cope. Though some of my fellow lecturers were supportive, I felt alone in my struggle. Mum treated me like the black sheep of the family. She didn't communicate with me while I was in Molepolole unless I phoned home. She ignored me.

Worse still, my employment at the college was not working. There was too much internal fighting, and I was getting sick of it all. The atmosphere was toxic and stifling. For my sanity and long-term well-being, I resigned from my job. I needed to find a suitable environment to heal. That environment, in the short term, was Australia.

I knew that Mum and Papa would not support my decision, and as expected, they were both livid. They argued I was making the wrong decision. Mum asked me why I couldn't just settle down like other children. She always compared me to my siblings, which I loathed. I stood my ground and listened to my instincts. If I stayed in that toxic home environment, I would go mad. Papa understood my decision, even though he did not like it.

Soon after, I sold most of my belongings to fund my trip back to Australia. However, I stayed in Botswana long enough to witness the birth of my first niece, Nelly's first child. She was a beautiful little girl. I left when she was ten days old. The sense of relief when I left was palpable. I planned to live in Australia to study for a Ph.D. then find a job in South Africa.

I found it harder to settle in Australia this time around. I had limited funds because I was no longer on a scholarship; I had given up a promising career and disappointed my parents with my decision to go back to Australia. I struggled and still had anxiety attacks. Doug and I got back together. Things did not get any better. A year later, I left the relationship for good.

After a few months of working in low-level admin-istrative jobs to make ends meet, I found a professional job teaching English to adult migrants. This was different from the high school and teacher training jobs I had in Botswana, but it enabled me to use my teaching skills. I worked for a good organisation with friendly, passionate staff. My anxiety disappeared. I put my study plan in motion and enrolled in a Ph.D.

One Saturday morning in March 1991, my flatmate Busile called out to me, "Anna, wake up, there's a telephone call for you from Botswana."

I rushed to the phone, wondering who it might be. My uncle was on the line. "Hello, Anna. I have sad news. Your Papa died last night."

The news of his passing came as a shock. I spoke to Mum and Kuki and told them I would fly back the following week. I arrived in Botswana the day before the funeral. Many relatives had turned up for the funeral. In Setswana culture, when someone dies, relatives gather at the home and stay until after the burial. His death sunk in when I arrived and saw all the relatives. I wept.

Papa's passing was the closing of a significant chapter of my life. I remember standing beside his grave, overcome by a deep sadness as I watched his casket being lowered to the ground. It hit me; I would never see him again.

The wonderful memories we had shared as a family came flooding back. More tears came.

I had hoped Papa's passing would put a lid on my anxiety and problems with relationships. It did not—the patterns were too ingrained.

CONTEXT AND REFLECTION

Despite having had the opportunity to redefine myself, I was still affected by the situation at home when I went back. The family tensions, arguments, and the shifted power dimensions between my parents opened the wound of trauma that permeated all aspects of my adult life resulting in anxiety and depression.

My personal life was not ideal. It seemed everything I tried did not work. In turn, this intensified my pattern of self-criticism and self-blame.

Chapter 11

A New Ray of Sunshine

"What is hope but a feeling of optimism, a thought that says things will improve, it won't always be bleak, there's a way to rise above the present circumstances. Hope is an internal awareness that you do not have to suffer forever, and that somehow, somewhere there is a remedy for despair that you will come upon if you can only maintain this expectancy in your heart."

—Wayne Dyer

I met Moran, my spouse, in late 1993, when I was 37 years old. I was lonely and had been hoping to meet a suitable partner. My biological clock was ticking, and I was growing concerned I might not have a child.

One afternoon, I was strolling to a local club with a buddy when a car pulled up, and a tall, slim African man stopped and greeted us. My friend knew him well. He introduced us. The man looked kind and humble. A few weeks prior, I had a powerful premonition about meeting someone.

The next time I saw Moran was on Christmas Eve at my friend's place. I had dropped in on my way to midnight mass as his apartment was close to the church.

"Oh, hello, we meet again. I remember you from a few weeks ago," I said. We had quite a pleasant conversation. Again, his calm personality and humility impressed me. I left for church.

Our next encounter was on New Year's Eve, at a dance in the Tin Sheds at Sydney University. I was with a group of friends, and he came over to join us. I was glad that he was there. We all parted ways in the wee hours of the morning.

The following day Moran rang to find out if I had arrived home okay. I thought that was nice. He invited me to join him and a group of people at a music festival in Bondi. I declined, as the previous night had exhausted me. Soon, he started ringing me just to chat.

One Sunday, I was on my way home from church when I ran into him at a shopping mall close to where he lived. My church was in that area. We chatted for a while, and he walked me halfway home. That is when I started having a sense that perhaps he was interested in having an affair with me.

A few days later, I invited him to my house for dinner. We talked at length, and I found him easy to converse with. During our conversation, he told me he had an eight-year-old son. He also told me he had separated from his wife. We started going out a few weeks later.

Our relationship moved slowly; we took the time to get to know each other better. Moran spent a lot of time at my place, and I eventually met his son. In the beginning, the relationship went well. We gave each other space. I was busy with my studies, and he had his commitments.

We moved in together a few months after we met. The relationship started being a challenge for me. I found it tough to cope with a blended relationship and the complications that come with it. However, we slowly worked through our issues.

As the relationship developed, I discovered we shared common interests. We loved adventure and travel and enjoyed excellent food and wine. We shared a common Christian faith.

I learned about and enjoyed Moran's quirky sense of humour and love of life. He has a positive outlook on life— he is a well-measured and compassionate person, likable, and easy to get along with. I very much admired his patience, a quality that up to then eluded me. I had a lot to learn from him, and I liked that.

Moran is a very private person and doesn't talk about his family much. However, he told me about his upbringing and growing up in a village in Zambia with his uncles and many cousins. He comes from a large, connected, extended family.

I became pregnant about six months after we moved in together, a delightful, unexpected surprise. I had almost given up on falling pregnant and having a family. I was over the moon. My dream of meeting someone and starting a family was coming true.

We moved from my small flat to a three-bedroom house in Roselands, a Sydney suburb, and life settled into a comfortable routine. The pregnancy was going well, and I started sensing the baby's movements and kicks. I was nineteen weeks pregnant when one morning, I noticed some spotting. Dread overcame me.

The bleeding increased, and I started getting cramps. Moran drove me to a nearby hospital. On the way, I prayed for the baby to be alright. We waited for the midwife to see us. By then, I had dilated and was bleeding even heavier. She informed us that the baby would not survive. I lost him a few hours later that afternoon. The little boy, Anthony, was the spitting image of his father.

His loss devastated us—the shock and pain of loss are indescribable. Organising his funeral was a heartbreaking experience. A part of me departed with him. I blamed myself for the loss, feeling guilty that I could not carry him to term.

A few weeks after losing Anthony, I saw a gynaecologist to investigate the cause of my recurring miscarriages. I received an unexpected and serious health diagnosis unrelated to the miscarriage. This new situation drove me into utter despair and helplessness. It tested my faith and sense of judgment. The hurt and humiliation threw me into depression.

After this experience, my conscience urged me to seek answers to heal my soul and understand why my dreams and aspirations were not coming to fruition. It was then that I stumbled onto Louise Hay's book, *You Can Heal Your Life*. My journey into self-help and self-healing began.

I was starved for information. I scrounged bookstores for self-help books and tapes, and I discovered a wide range of resources. All I read on the topic of self-help and self-healing seemed foreign to me. It was hard to grasp how to use my mental resources to influence my physical life. I did not know where to start. Still, I had hope.

Losing Anthony deadened my motivation to continue with my Ph.D. In 1994, I deferred it to deal with my grief. Sadly, I never returned to university to finish it.

Time passed, and I had been living with Moran for a couple of years; our relationship continued to strengthen. We agreed to move our relationship to the next level. I was ready to introduce him to my family.

Moran had already met Rose, who had visited Australia many times, and they struck a good rapport. However, I was nervous about introducing Moran to Mum, as she had never approved of my previous relationships. The few times I had brought a boyfriend home, she found something to dislike.

Nonetheless, we agreed he would accompany me on my next visit to Botswana, at the end of a project I was doing with some Technikon colleges in South Africa. We also talked about going to Zambia to meet his family.

HEADWINDS AHEAD

Two years after I met Moran, in 1995, my dear sister Kuki was diagnosed with cancer. She now had a spouse and had a four-year-old daughter. It was a sad and stressful time for the family.

I rang and spoke to her, "Kuki, stay strong. Are you getting a second opinion?"

"Yes, I'll consult another gynaecologist in Kanye. I think you should come back home."

"I cannot just pack up and come back, Kuki. I know this news is heartbreaking. I wish I could. It won't be easy to get a job, and I want to resume my studies."

It was a tough conversation. She tried to understand, but I sensed the desperation and dread in her voice. She worried about what would happen to her daughter if she passed on. I assured her everything would work out okay.

She received treatment in South Africa and travelled back and forth between Johannesburg and Botswana for chemotherapy and radiation. Despite the treatment, the cancer progressed. I saw her whenever I could when I travelled to South Africa for my project.

It was during this turbulent time, in early 1998, that I fell pregnant again much to my surprise. Moran and I were overjoyed, though a bit cautious. We hoped for the best. The pregnancy went well until I developed complications in the second trimester—this time, I miscarried at twenty-three weeks. We lost another precious little boy, Madiba. Another heart-breaking funeral had to be planned.

Madiba breathed in my arms for at least one hour before saying goodbye. He held on for that much longer, to bond with his Mummy. Goodbye, my brave little man. I watched them wheel him away in the little crib.

This loss brought me to the brink of a total mental meltdown. By the time his funeral came about, I had regular blinding headaches. My faith and the support of friends and colleagues helped get me through. However, the pain and thought of saying goodbye to another little soul stopped me in my tracks.

Further medical investigations revealed a medical cause of the miscarriages. The doctor informed me of the repercussions of trying to conceive again. It crushed me to give up my aspiration to be a Mum. In my mind, I had failed.

The road to healing was brutal and steep. On the outside, I looked ok, but inside I was a mess. I was rotting with a seething anger at myself and life. I saw a psychologist and started yoga and meditation. These tools helped me cope and begin to feel better about myself.

I was in South Africa in April 1999 when Mum rang to tell me that Kuki's illness was now at a terminal stage, and she was in hospital in Palapye.

Moran had flown in to spend time with me in South Africa, and he was to accompany me to Botswana to meet Mum and Kuki as earlier agreed. A few weeks later, we flew to Gaborone after I completed work on the project. We hired a car from Gaborone airport to travel north to Palapye, where Kuki lived, and when we arrived in Palapye, we drove straight to the hospital.

The sight of my sister frail and scared tore me apart inside. We held each other and cried. She was struggling to accept the situation.

When Kuki met Moran, they hit it off straight away. I left them talking while I spoke to Kuki's doctor, who advised that they were discharging her that evening and wanted to meet with the family the following day.

Moran and I drove Kuki home from the hospital, and we found Mum there, with Kuki's husband and daughter. Mum had just arrived from Francistown, and to my surprise, she was very personable when she met Moran.

After the introductions, Moran and I walked to the nearby shopping mall to buy drinks and snacks. We returned and sat with Mum in the living room while Kuki was resting. I took this opportunity for a formal introduction.

"Mum, Moran comes from Zambia, in the Southern Province, around Livingstone," I said.

"Oh, I know the area well. I used to be a nurse in Kasane, a village in Botswana's northern tip close to Zambia. I used to cross over at Kazungula to take patients to Livingstone hospital. I liked the people there. They were all very kind to me," Mum said to Moran, beaming. They had struck a rapport.

"My family comes from Monze, a small town along the main transport corridor between Livingstone and Lusaka," Moran replied.

Mum turned and looked at me, a radiant smile on her face. "It's a pity you two are not staying long. I'm going to the cattle post in a few weeks. I would like to give Moran a goat as a present."

Wow, that was a huge surprise coming from Mum. In our culture, presenting someone with livestock is an enormous honour. Mum had taken over running the cattle post when Papa passed on. I knew her offering Moran a goat was a symbolic gesture and sign of approval—I was dumbfounded!

"Thank you," Moran said, surprised. "That's very similar to my culture. My family are farmers too, and livestock is very important to us. I appreciate that very much."

"Thanks, Mum. That's a lovely gesture," I said.

Mum had no issues with me sharing a room with Moran. Another first! Her acceptance of Moran was an enormous morale booster for me. It signified a new direction in my relationship with her. I was delighted that she accepted Moran. Her approval of him made my stay far more comfortable this time, despite the sad and sombre occasion of Kuki's prognosis.

The following morning Mum, Kuki, and I met with the doctor. I remember how resigned my poor sister looked as the doctor discussed her situation. The oncologist's report from Johannesburg stated the cancer had metastasised, and no further treatment was available for her. Six months of survival was the most optimistic prognosis. The finality of it all crushed me.

We decided Kuki would travel with Mum and us to Francistown to spend a week together. Moran and I would drive her back to Palapye on our way to Gaborone. Her husband stayed in Palapye with her daughter, who was attending school. We loaded up the rental car we hired upon arrival, and Moran drove us to Francistown.

When we reached Francistown, Mum wanted to take Kuki to visit spiritual healers. Kuki became very distressed, and they started arguing.

"They will help you," Mum fretted. "They told me they would help you!"

"I told you I don't believe in those things. Can you leave me alone?" Kuki shouted at her.

"Mum, stop!" I boomed. She looked at me, shocked by the strength of my voice. "Let her be. Please stop!"

Mum hesitated. I could see her struggling with the situation. She tried to argue, but I was having none of it. She gave up and left us alone in the room. I asked Kuki what she wanted to talk about.

She stared at me, "This is serious, you know. I'm dying."

I fought back tears as I told her I knew. Deep sorrow and compassion towards her overwhelmed me. She understood the gravity of what she was facing. The most I could do was give her the space to deal with it as best as she could.

I held her hand. "What can I do to support you?"

We discussed many personal wishes, some of which I couldn't later fulfil for legal reasons.

After a week in Francistown, Moran and I drove her back to Palapye on our way to Gaborone to catch the flight to Sydney. I planned to arrange for three months' leave to go back to Botswana.

It tore me apart to say goodbye to her that morning. She had mothered me and given me so much support throughout my life. She was with me for every triumph and tribulation and never once failed me. I was leaving her behind, hoping to see her again soon. The trip to Gaborone and back to Australia was rough. I was so glad I had Moran with me.

I kept in touch with Mum to see how Kuki was doing. Mum told me Kuki returned to Francistown a few days after we left her in Palapye because she was not feeling well, and Mum was caring for her.

Two weeks after I arrived back in Sydney, on the 9th June 1999, my cousin called me to tell me that Kuki had passed on. I was deflated, but I stayed calm as I asked what time she died. Then I sat and prayed.

I left for Botswana two days later. My sister Rose and I met in Johannesburg and flew to Gaborone together. We met with Cecil at Gaborone airport and hired a car to drive to Palapye, where Kuki's funeral was to take place.

When I arrived at her house, I felt a powerfully strong sense of her presence. I dashed out of the house to contain myself. Her spirit was there with me.

Cecil came out to console me. "Did you just sense her?"

I nodded. I missed her so much. My beautiful, loving sister was no longer there.

Her funeral was gut-wrenching. It was strange to see her body lowered to the ground. I knew she had similar scars to what I carried. Sometimes we had talked about those hard times in our childhood. But then, she would reassure me they were over, and we have moved on. It broke me into a million pieces to see her beloved daughter so lost in grief. I held her close to me through the funeral ceremony.

After returning to Australia, I struggled to cope. I needed something to hold on to. That's when I discovered the *Tibetan Book of Living and Dying*, which outlined the Buddhist belief of spiritually helping people who have died. I followed the suggested daily practice for forty-nine days to help her along her journey. At the end of the period, I experienced tremendous calm.

One morning, when I was in the shower, I felt her spirit in the room. I sensed her peace. This time happiness replaced the usual urge to weep. I still speak to her today. She was a stalwart influence on my life, and though we fought like cat and mouse, our bond was solid, and our love for each other unshakable.

NEW HOPE

Over time, life returned to normal after the struggle to deal with Kuki's passing. My relationship with Moran was solid and going well, and his support helped me to move on.

After Kuki's death, I visited Botswana every year to see Mum. During these trips, we had in-depth discussions about my life in Australia and my childhood difficulties.

"Mum, I need you to understand why I returned to Australia," I said one evening after dinner. "I found the situation at home traumatic. Things had changed a lot in

Botswana, and when I became sick, I was unsupported. I left Botswana for my sanity. I was drowning."

"Were you that unwell? You could have sought help here," she said, defensively.

"No, Mum, the stress was unsustainable. There was too much tension between us. The stressful atmosphere at home has always affected me from a young age. I hated the violence."

"What tension? We raised you with a lot of love."

"This is the problem, Mum. Whenever I bring up issues, you either deny them or dismiss me. I'm grown-up now and won't accept this treatment from you."

Her eyes flashed with anger, but she backed off.

I continued, "Also, Mum, I was destroyed by how you and Papa treated me when I miscarried in Lobatse. I have struggled for years to recover from that. You rejected me and threatened to disown me."

"I admit we handled that really bad, Anna. Things have not always been easy at home since you were little. But I have always had your best interests at heart. I did the best I could."

"I understand, Mum. However, you need to understand that I love Australia; I have relative peace there and have now made it my home."

"You mean you will never come back home?" she looked shocked.

"Maybe, subject to Moran agreeing to move."

"But I need you to look after Benny when I'm gone. You know he is struggling."

"Mum, you have always known about Benny's struggles. You did nothing. It's unfair to expect us to uproot our lives to come and look after him. He needs professional help. We'll do the best we can."

It was hard for her to hear the truth. We disagreed about Benny. My brother had his own life. Like myself, he had his mental challenges, but he was doing ok.

Mum passed on in 2001. I flew to Botswana for her funeral. It hurt to say goodbye to her. She had been a significant, dominant figure in our lives, and it was strange to imagine life without her. Her passing was the end of an era. We no longer had our parents to look up to.

I remember Moran shaking me awake one morning in early September, a few weeks after Mum's passing. "Wake up, America is being attacked!"

"What do you mean?" I sleepily wasn't able to figure out what he was talking about.

"Come and watch what's on TV."

I scrambled out of bed and rushed to the TV. I'll never forget the confronting images of people covered in dust and smoke billowing from buildings.

"Oh, my God! We're scheduled to fly to London in ten days!" I said, my hand on my mouth.

"Yep, I know."

"I'll call the travel agent when I get to work to clarify."

We were to join a three-week tour of several countries in Europe from London. We were looking forward to the trip after months of planning. I needed a break to recover after Mum's recent passing. The travel agent assured me the trip was still going ahead as scheduled when I rang that morning.

Though a crisis happened in the United States, we did, indeed, carry on with our travel plans. The flight to London included a few days' stopover in Singapore. It was hilarious to see Moran spend almost half of our holiday savings on camera equipment. He loved shopping in Singapore and was behaving like a kid in a toy store. He bought lots of clothes he never ended up wearing, except for one fake, tailored Armani jacket, which he still wears. We loved the holiday. We spent time with Rose after we finished the tour.

In late November, Moran and I flew from London to Francistown for a family reunion, to perform a traditional ceremony three months after Mum's passing. Moran and I spent the time renovating and preparing Mum's house for the ceremony. We had invited relatives from both sides of my family.

Rose flew from the UK soon after we left Europe, and she helped us with the preparations for the ceremony. Nelly and her then spouse helped where they could, in between running their businesses. Cecil and Benny attended the ceremony. Many of our relatives were there. Mum's church group, the Saint Anna women, attended, which was a great honour in her memory. This event was a significant period of reflection. It was a purging of the past.

After the ceremony, Moran, Rose, and I stayed back to complete renovations on Mum's house to prepare for renting it out. Cecil, Benny, and Nelly all went back to their respective homes. At Christmas time, Nelly and her husband invited Rose, Moran, and me to visit Kasane and the Chobe National park for a couple of days of wildlife viewing. It was a fantastic family trip with lots of wonderful memories.

We completed most of the house renovations in early January 2002, and Moran and I flew to Zambia so I could meet his family for the first time. Moran's younger brothers Colin, Phil, Lawrie, and his cousin Jane met us at the airport. Moran's parents had passed a long while before. I marvelled at how connected the family was.

We stayed with his cousin Jane in Lusaka, the capital city of Zambia. His brothers organised a party to welcome him home after being away for eighteen years. Many of his relatives came. It was a gracious gesture for them to show such a level of support for their brother. They welcomed me with open arms, and all called me "*Mulamu*," which means in-law.

I felt at home. Moran's family network was expansive, which surprised me, given that he did not talk much about them.

CHANGE OF SCENERY

In 2002 Moran got a job in Bahrain, and we moved there. The change of scenery was welcome. After living together for ten years, we formally got married before leaving for Bahrain.

Our wedding took place on a sunny winter afternoon on the 27th of July. It was a small but beautiful ceremony.

My perspective changed when we got married—for the first time, I felt truly stable and grounded. I made the silent commitment to myself to do the mental work required to understand my problems and heal my mind.

Moran left for Bahrain in November 2002; I was to follow three months later. On the 30th of December 2002, a couple of months before I left Australia for Bahrain, my brother Cecil died in a car accident in Zimbabwe. This was horrible news. For logistical reasons connected with my imminent departure for Bahrain, I could not attend his funeral.

I remember well how awful it was not to attend his burial. On the day of his funeral, two of my friends accompanied me to attend mass at St Mary's Cathedral in Sydney.

Cecil's death devastated me. We were just starting to spend more time with each other and get to know each other well. Cecil was ten years older than me, and we never had a chance to know each other well when we were growing up. He was away most of the time in our adult lives. However, I was incredibly grateful that he had visited me in Sydney for New Year's celebration in 2000, and we had a brilliant time together. We also got to talk about our aspirations. He was great company.

I took leave without pay from my job and left for Bahrain in March 2003 during the peak of the second gulf war. Bahrain was nothing like I had imagined. It was sandy and hot, with few trees or greenery. It was very humid.

"Gosh, I hope it doesn't get any hotter than this!" I said to Moran.

He laughed, "Wait until the summer!" During hot months, the average temperature in the region would be around 45°centigrade, sometimes even hotter.

We endured the extreme relentless sun and heat for over six months in a year. The air conditioning was on round the clock. Sometimes, we woke up to find the house full of dust seeping through the air conditioning ducts after severe dust storms.

After my first horrific experience of the Bahrain summer, I travelled during the hot months. I visited Rose in the UK and sometimes Nelly and Benny in Botswana. Moran stayed back because of work commitment.

Bahraini culture fascinated us. The locals kept to themselves and did not mix much with expatriates. Though the dominant language is Arabic, most people spoke English. Bahrain was quite liberal and modern, and expatriates lived a free life compared to other countries in the region. However, we had to respect the rules of Muslim society.

We moved to Awali, a compound occupied by expatriate workers about twenty kilometres away from Manama, the major town centre. Awali was a pleasant area to live, with comfortable houses and good security. We met fellow expatriates from the UK, New Zealand, The Philippines, South Africa, and fellow Australians. Life in Bahrain was slow and relaxed. I soon became strong and back to my normal self.

When we returned to Sydney three years later, we had changed. For one, our outlook on life was a lot more relaxed. The immersion into a different culture and social environment was very refreshing and enriching.

I resumed my old job when we returned to Australia. I enjoyed integrating back into the professional life of working with diverse students in a busy environment. Life took on a relaxed pace. I was much more settled and coping well but continued my work to support myself and heal my emotional wounds.

One of my friends, a Buddhist, rang me one morning. "Would you like to visit the temple with me tomorrow?" she asked.

I agreed though I knew little about Buddhism. I drove to her house on Saturday morning, and she drove us to the temple. The temple was full of monks in bright orange apparel, kneeling and chanting in Vietnamese, in front of a colossal statue of the Buddha. The repetitive chanting awoke a deep spiritual chord within me. It soothed me. Even though I did not understand what they were saying, it comforted me. My adventure into Buddhism had begun—another opportunity to fortify my spirituality.

I started studying Buddhism as a healing philosophy and way of life in 2017. Its practical approach to life's challenges drew me. I liked its teaching of practical skills, like mindful meditation, to enable people to transform their life experiences and assume responsibility and control over their lives.

Buddhism provided me with the answers I needed at a deeper level; it helped me get in touch with my inner-self. It provided me with tools on how to eliminate suffering and achieve happiness in life. Through Buddhism, I learned suffering originates from a deluded mentality, which results in negative and unhealthy states of mind. These unhealthy states of mind may lead to psychological afflictions such as anxiety, borderline personality disorders, and depression.

I learned I could cultivate self-awareness through the practice of mindfulness to achieve the "right view" of life— this was right up my alley. I craved to learn more, and a window to my mind started opening. The beginnings of clarity were chomping at my heels! I was doing very well.

ANOTHER BLOW

In 2018, Moran, my "Prince of Mpondoland" as he called himself, was diagnosed with a life-threatening illness. He had been unwell for some time. During that period, he had been undergoing multiple medical tests to find out the cause of his health issue.

One morning he rang me at work. He had gone for a CT scan that morning. "The haematologist has just called. He wants to see me today."

A bolt of fear jolted through me. I shoved the nerves down. "I'm sure it will be ok. Did he say why?"

"No, he just sounded like it's urgent."

"Okay," I replied, with as much calm as I could muster, "Let me know how you go."

Moran rang me an hour later to let me know he had Hodgkin's lymphoma. The hospital wanted to start treatment as soon as possible since the lymphoma was already in an advanced stage. Shock coursed through my body. I fought to stay calm. Powerful sensations of dread churned in my stomach. I felt like spewing. I rushed home from work. We hugged and held onto each other.

"We'll get through this," he said, calmly. "I have to prepare myself for the challenge ahead."

His calm resolve was reassuring. I have always admired Moran's mental strength, but even more so at that moment.

Moran's treatment schedule coincided with a planned family reunion in Botswana. Rose, Moran, and I were to travel to Botswana to lay new tombstones on Mum, Papa, Cecil, and Kuki's graves. We had no option but to cancel the trip and defer the tombstone laying ceremony to a future date.

The treatment started two weeks after diagnosis. It was a difficult and stressful period for me as a primary carer. I feared the worst but held on tight and supported him through his treatment. He was a real trooper and fought as hard as he could. Moran had a strong resilience and a positive outlook throughout, despite enduring horrific side effects. The chemotherapy and immune booster drugs knocked him around. We both held on to our faith.

The role of a carer is harrowing. I was responsible for synthesising the doctor's instructions, including prescriptions, appointments, and progress reports. Moran could not absorb all this information, let alone remember it. I had to stay strong for him. It was not an easy feat for someone who had endured previous episodes of anxiety and depression.

I ran all the errands myself, including driving him to treatment sessions and doctor's appointments. Jason, my stepson, sometimes took him if I was unavailable. To see Moran fight a battle like that was humbling. I was helpless and sad. Through accompanying him for treatment, I developed a deep respect and compassion for people who have to endure this journey in their lives.

Moran completed his treatment in late December 2018. It was a tough journey, but he got through it. Rose came to visit in early January 2019 to support us. She has always been a supportive sister through tough times and happy times. We could count on her. Rose and Moran get along well, and I know her visit touched him deeply. We received messages of support from his family members in Zambia and from Nelly and her kids in Botswana. We pulled through with God's grace.

The strain of caring for Moran and facing uncertainty took its toll on my mental health. After many years of being okay, I sank back down into the hole of depression and anxiety. This time the anxiety attacks presented themselves via weird physical symptoms.

On one occasion, I saw a cardiologist because I experienced dizziness and heart palpitations. The cardiologist ordered some tests. I arrived at the cardiologist's rooms and waited.

"You may come in," the nurse said.

My heart leapt out of my chest. You've got heart problems. And you'll end up dying in your sixties like Papa. These thoughts swirled as the nurse prepared me for the angiogram. My heart had never worried me before. Yet today, somehow, everything was a big deal. *What the hell*, I remember jolting myself awake! My critical inner voice rang clear and loud! I reassured myself that I would be ok.

"All done. The heart muscle is ok, no issues there," the nurse said after the test.

My relief was tangible. I realised the palpitations and dizziness were part of the anxiety.

On another occasion, I ended up in hospital for severe abdominal pains. I started taking antidepressants to help me through this rough patch.

These experiences, nasty as they were, helped me grow. They helped me realise I was still holding onto many unhealthy underlying beliefs and habits.

I blamed the universe for what was happening in our lives. I became aware of how dependent I had become on Moran for my happiness and completeness. The thought of him not making it threw me overboard. I had to change this.

I started further mental work through prayer, affirmations, meditation, and yoga, this time with more determination and conviction.

2019 ended on a high note. Moran was now in remission. As part of the healing process, I suggested to Moran that we take a summer vacation to spend Christmas in Europe with Rose—the trip I described in the preamble.

CONTEXT AND REFLECTION

The positive events in my life gave me hope and optimism and the belief that things could work out if I cultivated self-awareness and worked toward releasing the underlying beliefs that triggered anxiety and depression.

I also realised that although it is not easy, mental and emotional healing is a long-term process and gets easier with growing awareness and continued practice.

Chapter 12

My Approach to Healing

Walking your "why" is the art of living your own personal set of values—the beliefs and behaviours you hold dear and give you a sense of meaning and satisfaction. Identifying and acting on the values that are truly your own- not those imposed on you by others, not what you think you 'should' care about, but what you genuinely do care about—is the crucial next step of achieving emotional agility.

—Susan David

One Monday afternoon, a teacher at a new teaching centre I managed organised a welcome lunch for me. The staff and I were sitting around a large rectangular table. The conversation came around to children.

"Have you got any children?" One staff member asked me.

"No, I don't." There was an awkward silence.

Eyes burned into me. Discomfort and embarrassment were rising. "I tried but was unsuccessful. I'm a stepmom."

"Oh, that's okay." There was a swift change of subject to something else. I felt embarrassed, guilty, and inadequate.

Sometimes I was still self-conscious about not having a biological child. The roots of this were embedded in my cultural upbringing, where it was an expectation that women should become mothers—women who don't are considered lacking. Some people treated me differently when I disclosed I didn't have children of my own. I found this cruel.

Some women don't have children, and this is due to various reasons. Most times, like my situation, it's not a lifestyle choice. For me, the stigma associated with not having children solidified my internal belief that I was not good enough, which, in turn, diminished my successes in other areas of my life.

What is it that held me back? Was it fear? I discovered that my underlying self-limiting beliefs contributed a lot to this. As Mike Dooley says in *Infinite Possibilities: The Art of Living Your Dreams*, "To master your thoughts and imagination, and therefore your life and destiny, you must first master their captain-your beliefs."

As I became able to filter out the noise of my self-critical voice, I gained enough mental clarity to realise and understand some of the deeply rooted beliefs behind my thoughts. Finding this clarity unlocked the door to changing my outlook.

I discovered an underlying assumption that caused me a reluctance to challenge other people's views. I feared that if I displeased people, they would reject and abandon me, which I internalized to mean that I wasn't good enough and not worth loving. I also discovered my underlying need for other people's approval.

When I was growing up, women had limited rights in my culture. Men controlled them, and it was generally un-acceptable for a woman to seek independence. Men beat their wives when they expressed independence, and the culture accepted this. I chose to buck social norms; at university in Botswana, I was independent and enjoyed socialising with male friends, often sharing a drink and a smoke.

One day, one guy asked me, "Don't you ever consider getting married?"

"Of course, I do. What do you mean?"

"Don't you think drinking will scare guys away?"

Embarrassed, I brushed him off. I did not challenge him. But I was hurt and felt he was saying I was not good enough to marry.

My response to him—and throughout my younger years—stemmed from my beliefs about women's status in society. I did not grow up with a good reference point for strong, independent women. I had always been resentful of Mum for staying in an abusive relationship; I felt she had not been an exemplary role model for us girls.

When I discussed this with her, she told me she had limited choices in those days. She tried to get help from the local police chief, but he dismissed her, saying he did not want to get involved.

This made me furious. It explained Mum's internalised anger and passive-aggressiveness. She had no power. The unwillingness of others to help a woman in an abusive situation explained her lack of friends and support. She preferred to keep her lot to herself—a significant burden to carry. It also explained where I got a distorted view of myself.

Recovering, standing solidly on my own feet, and disempowering depression has been a long and messy journey.

The Buddha said, "When the student is ready, the teacher will appear." Teachers appear in our lives in many forms, at different stages of our lives. I discovered many teachers along the way, through books, meditation and yoga, hypnotherapy, self-hypnosis, and through friends and family.

Positive affirmations are great in helping me to counter negative thoughts. Medication has come in handy to lessen the acute effects of anxiety attacks and treat symptoms of the depression that has plagued me most of my life. However, it does not address the underlying thought patterns and beliefs that often trigger episodes. I am not advocating against medication; it is often an important element of the healing journey.

In my case, however, I don't believe reliance on long-term medication will resolve my issues. I think relying on medication in the long term would rob me of the opportunity to find my strengths and my ability to utilise my internal resources to heal myself.

My husband, Moran, has been my teacher. Through his gentle, non-judgmental eyes, I discover hidden parts of myself, which always helps me grow. I learned how to set boundaries in a relationship, which was a very significant step for me. As we move forward together, I realise that healthy relationships rely on give-and-take and provide a rich opportunity to grow and become wiser.

Through meditation, I gained clarity about who I am. I started seeing the plethora of rules, regulations, dos and don'ts, judgments, and conditions that were strangling my life! The turning point for me came with the internal decision to change my outlook and begin believing in myself. Change is fundamental for healing and growth.

I had to view life from a different, more realistic perspective. Though I cannot pinpoint the exact moment I changed, losing little Madiba solidified that decision. I needed to stop being defeated by life, viewing my experiences through the same obscure lens. There had to be a better way.

I realised that every time I experienced an emotional upheaval, I fell back into anxiety and depression. This pattern showed me I was not challenging and changing the root cause of the problem. I knew I had to deal with this.

Born into a Catholic family, I grew up with deep faith, even though I haven't always practised my faith throughout my life. However, faith has been a significant support for me. Whenever I am in deep despair, I look to God, and God walks with me and helps me shoulder the daily burdens. In faith, I found hope and peace. I find talking to God a very rewarding and empowering experience—things become less hopeless. I still experience major challenges, but I can withstand them.

I do regular mirror work, repeating positive messages to myself in the mirror, to reveal my own internalised negative patterns and change them. I go inside and muster the courage to scrutinise my thought patterns.

I know my place in life and have stopped comparing myself to others. The focus on my considerable strengths gives me joy. It gives me peace of mind.

Creativity—writing this book—is one of those strengths. I challenge my negative thoughts and fact check them, and call them out to be untrue. This technique has helped me to view life and its challenges more realistically and stop the self-criticism.

I learned to live in the present, giving myself the love I crave. I am open to making choices without needing the world to validate them before they feel justifiable and acceptable.

I no longer fear vulnerability—in my vulnerability lies my strength, flexibility, and malleability. I am open to new learning and different points of view.

CONTEXT AND REFLECTION

For many years a deeply seated belief of not being good enough dominated my life, which, in turn, led to negative, unfortunate consequences.

Self-help strategies like meditation, hypnotherapy, mirror work, and affirmations helped me heal and let go of the trauma that caused anxiety and depression. This internal work is ongoing.

I now firmly believe what Wayne Dyer states below.

> *You cannot send problems out of your life by attacking them or understanding them in more depth. Instead, you correct the error in your thinking that produces the problem in the first place. Once you bring a correction to the problem it no longer has any substance or validity, and it disappears completely from your life.*

Chapter 13

Conclusion

Throughout this book, I've shared my story of living with low-level depression for most of my life, ultimately leading me to seek answers to help myself heal.

Diagnosis and treatment of these and other mental disorders were uncommon in the 50s and 60s in Botswana, particularly for children. Society dismissed the outward expression of these disorders as rebelliousness and refusal to conform.

In my own family, some often regarded my mental struggles as embarrassing rebelliousness that brought shame.

I grew up as one of those people who swept their suffering under the rug, fearing society's judgment and ignorance when faced with the reality of my mental health. I also did not want to cause any more embarrassment for my family.

Change, for me, was difficult. It was a protracted process triggered by frightening episodes of anxiety and depression. However, once I began to change and understood that I could choose to view my situation differently, the actual work of healing commenced through a combination of psycho-therapeutic intervention and self-help strategies.

I uncovered ingrained limiting beliefs that drove my life decisions and choices. To cultivate growth and balance my life, I needed to continue releasing these limitations.

I learned many lessons along the path of self-change and discovery. Self-change is a lifelong exercise—I realised I need to practice self-compassion as I continue to learn. I discovered the biggest bully is my mind!

There's a point at which we all can make a turn for the better, where we promise ourselves that we'll step up to the mark and be the best version of ourselves no matter what happens. Once we reach that point, the innate self knows it will be ok despite the rough road ahead.

Understanding and embracing this idea led to the clarity I sought all my life. The light within became the driving force in my life.

Keep seeking and believing that you will find your light, and you will! I wanted to share this story, hoping that something about my healing journey will trigger something on your own road of self-healing.

You have within you the absolute ability to increase your frequency and enhance the energy field of your everyday life. By increasing the speed at which you vibrate you move into those frequencies I'm calling spirit, and away from those that are grounded in the material world of problems.

—Wayne Dyer

Epilogue

Despite my life circumstances, I am still standing—many positive things are happening in my world, and I have a wonderful rapport with my remaining family members.

I still hold deep memories of my childhood and my relationship with my parents and siblings. I wonder how my life would be if Mum, Papa, my brother Cecil and my sister Kuki were still alive.

I've come to accept that Mum and Papa did only what they thought best in their circumstances. I know my existence has a purpose and that my journey, though challenging, is not random and has enriched me.

I believe we all are on particular learning paths through life.

BENNY

My brother Benny grew up as a handsome and outgoing child. In his youth, he had many talents. He was a gifted guitarist and used to sometimes play with visiting bands in Francistown. He played tennis for his university team. He was a high school teacher and took early retirement.

Benny has mental challenges and difficulties. However, his strength and resilience keep him going in his own way.

After the incident with the maid, Mmamoritshana, when Benny was little, Mum became overprotective of him, to the extent where she expected us to do everything for him. To date, Benny expects other people to look after him. He still lives in Francistown.

ROSE

My sister Rose grew up independent and has carried this independence throughout her life.

She lives in the UK, and we strive to see each other often. She is a loving, kind soul, and very successful in her chosen career path in the medical field.

She, Moran, and I often travel to many parts of the world together. We are very close and share a similar, positive outlook on living. Rose has visited me in Australia many times. She has been a solid, reliable support for Moran and me over the years.

NELLY

Nelly, the youngest one in the family, still lives in Botswana. Like my other siblings, we grew up close.

She has been to Australia to visit us on a couple of occasions. We are in constant touch and plan to spend more time together as a family soon.

Nelly also took up a teaching career—I guess we were all following in Papa's footsteps.

She is a lovely, calm person and is fantastic with people. Nelly, a devoted mum, was determined to give her three children—two girls and a boy—the best upbringing possible. She is also a dedicated grandmother.

She enjoys a relaxed lifestyle in Francistown.

MORAN

Moran is a keen photographer and is now actively collating memories from our diverse travels into a photobook. Together, we are looking forward to the next adventure in a new, exotic part of the world.

Our relationship continues to develop in exciting and positive directions. He's a great support, and through our relationship, I continue to grow and learn more about myself and my resilience. His understanding of my life challenges provides the anchor that I need to heal.

As for myself, I have endured many challenges in my life, like a palm tree being battered by a hurricane. Through it all, I have found the strength and resilience to bounce back like a palm tree—palm trees are flexible and can bend to the point of being horizontal to the ground during storms, but they don't break.

When the storm dies down, the palm tree stands upright again.

I hope you, too, can find the strength to stand upright again after enduring severe storms in your life.

THE END

Resources

Fung Kei Cheng and Samson Tse. Journal of Religion & Spirituality in Social Work. Social Thought, Volume 34, 2015. Issue 1

David, S. *Emotional Agility: Get Unstuck, Embrace Change and Thrive in Work and Life.* Penguin Life. UK. 2017

Dooley, M. *Infinite Possibilities: The Art of Living Your Dreams.* Atria Paperback. New York London Toronto Sydney. 2009

Dyer, W. *There's A Spiritual Solution to Every Problem.* HarperCollins Publishers. Sydney. Australia. 2001

Fulton, P.R. and Siegel, R. D. (2005) 'Buddhist and Western Psychology, Seeking Common Ground' in *Mindfulness and Psychotherapy*, Second Edition, edited by Christopher Germer et al, Chapter 2, pages 36 - 56, Guilford Press.

Lewis Herman, J. Trauma and Recovery: The Aftermath of Violence- From Domestic Abuse to Political Terror. https://www.goodreads.com/work/quotes/530025-trauma-and-recovery

Rinpoche, S. *The Tibetan Book of Living and Dying.* Rider London. 1992

Rusk, T. *Mind Traps: Change Your Mind Change Your life.* Thorson London 1988

Sumedho, A. *The Four Noble Truths.* Amaravati. Hertfordshire, 1992

Applying the Buddhist Four Immeasurables to Mental Health Care: A Critical Review.

Wallace, A. *The Boundless Heart: The Cultivation of the Four Immeasurables.* Snow Lion. New York. 1999

Acknowledgements

I would like to acknowledge and express my gratitude to the following:

My dear husband, who became the beta reader for this book and gave me honest feedback while supporting me all the way. Without his input, this book would not have turned out to be what it is today. I'm grateful for your suggestions and the time you spent reviewing the manuscript.

My editor, Amy Colvin, who gave me valuable feedback and support and encouragement throughout the editing process. Thank you for making my writing journey so much easier and attainable.

My dear sisters, who helped with fact-checking and validation of family events. Thank you for your positivity and support in writing this book.

About the Author

Anna Choongo has many years of experience as a teacher and manager in Australia and overseas. She has a master's degree in Applied Linguistics (TESOL), obtained from the University of Sydney. She also has a Bachelor of Education. Anna is an experienced presenter and speaker. She has facilitated multiple workshops throughout her career. She is keen on self-help and self-healing. She also loves travelling and spending time with family and friends.

Can You Help?

Thank you for reading my book!

I truly appreciate all of your feedback and would love to hear what you have to say. Your input will help me make the next version of this book and my future books better.

Please leave an honest review on Amazon, letting me know what you thought of the book.

Thanks so much!

Anna Choongo